# ABC<sup>s</sup> *of* Divorce *for* Women

# ABCs *of* Divorce *for* Women

## Carol Ann WILSON
CFP®, CDS

*and*

## Ginita WALL
CPA, CFP®, CDS

We've done our best to give you useful and accurate information in this book, but laws and regulations change frequently. Although this book is written by professionals, it should not be utilized as a substitute for professional services in specific situations. Consult with legal and financial professionals to make sure that facts and general advice contained in this book are applicable to your situation.

The authors gratefully acknowledge permission from ABA Publishing, to reprint several tables. All tables are current as of March 2002. Source: © The American Bar Association. All rights reserved. http://www.abanet.org/family/familylaw/tables.html.

First Printing 2003

Copyright © by Carol Ann Wilson and Ginita Wall

Cover Design by Mikell Yamada

Library of Congress Catalog Card Number: 90-91811

ISBN 0-9626790-5-4

Printed in the United States

Published by Quantum Press
6395 Gunpark Drive, Suite Y
Boulder, CO 80301
303-527-3193
866-527-3193

# ABOUT THE AUTHORS

## Carol Ann Wilson, CFP®, CDS

Carol Ann Wilson is a recognized specialist in marital financial issues and a pioneer in the field of divorce financial planning. Her pre-divorce financial consulting company, Quantum Financial, Inc. has been in business since 1986. She founded the Institute for Certified Divorce Planners in 1993 and is currently the President of the College for Divorce Specialists which trains lawyers, accountants and financial professionals in the financial issues in divorce. She designed software used by these organizations to calculate financially equitable divorce settlements. She has also served as an expert witness in court in over 100 divorce cases nationwide.

Wilson is the author of *The Financial Guide to Divorce Settlement*, and co-author of *The Survival Manual for Women in Divorce*, *The Survival Manual for Men in Divorce*, and *The Dollars and Sense of Divorce*.

She has appeared on the Regis Philbin Show, Geraldo, LifeTime Live, CNBC Financial News and numerous radio programs.

She frequently serves as a speaker and faculty member of high-ranking legal and financial organizations and has been published in numerous professional journals.

Carol Ann lives in Boulder, CO with her husband, Bill Fullmer. For further information, visit *www.carolannwilson.com* or *www.cdsCollege.com*. Email her at *carolann@carolannwilson.com* or call 303-527-3321.

### Ginita Wall, CPA, CFP®, CDS

As a nationally recognized expert on money, Ginita Wall is a frequent speaker for conventions, professional meetings, women's groups and philanthropic organizations. Named one of the 250 top financial advisors in the country by *Worth Magazine* for the past seven years, she has authored six books and three booklets on personal finance, including *Your Next Fifty Years*, a retirement guide for Baby Boomers, and *150 Ways to Divorce Without Going Broke*. She specializes in helping people through life transitions, including divorce and widowhood.

Co-founder of the non-profit Women's Institute for Financial Education (WIFE.org) and originator of the acclaimed Second Saturday program ("What Women Need to Know About Divorce"), she is a financial expert and columnist for iVillage.com, CNBC.com, Cox Interactive Media, as well as an advisor for the General Electric Center for Financial Learning and *Divorce Magazine*.

Ginita is quoted frequently in *The Wall Street Journal*, *USA Today*, *Business Week, Money,* and other financial publications, and she has appeared on the *NBC Nightly News*, *National Public Radio*, *CBS This Morning*, the Discovery Channel's *Home Matters*, and numerous other radio and television broadcasts. She is also listed in *Who's Who in Finance*.

Based in San Diego, Ginita Wall received her B.A. from Antioch College in Ohio, and she is a Certified Public Accountant in New Mexico and California. For further information, visit www.WIFE.org and www.planforwealth.com. Email her at Gwall@planforwealth.com or call (858) 792-0524.

# CONTENTS

# FOREWORD

Each year nearly 2.8 million people go through the emotional and financial trauma of divorce. The average length of a marriage that ends in divorce is less than ten years.

During divorce, many women are concerned about financial survival. Studies show that in the first year after divorce, the wife's standard of living drops almost 27 percent while the husband's increases by as much as 10 percent.

Many factors combine to lower women's standard of living after divorce. Caring for children can be expensive, and child support is often inadequate to cover the true costs of childrearing. The demands of motherhood prevent many women from pursuing high-powered careers.

Also, traditional conceptions of gender roles can lead women to choose careers that are less lucrative than their husbands'. The wife may become an elementary school teacher, while the husband becomes a college professor. After divorce, his earning power will far exceed hers.

The higher the income of the family, the wider the gap between the partners. This is because many high-income couples invest in the husband's career while the wife's takes second place. If the marriage lasts a long time, the wife can lose many important years of career growth, making it difficult for her to get back on her feet after divorce.

Unfortunately, many courts don't recognize career assets, such as education, seniority, industry contacts, and potential earning power, during property division. If the wife doesn't get a good settlement during divorce, she often has trouble making up the difference later. At the same time, courts expect both spouses to recover quickly from divorce. If alimony is awarded, it is often just a few years of "rehabilitative maintenance."

Over the years, we've seen some heartrending cases:

- Barbara, age 53, had never worked outside the home. She agreed to accept only three years of alimony after thirty years of marriage. She spent two years training at a local vocational school, then went out to look for work in her new field. Because of her age and her lack of experience in the workforce, she had great difficulty finding a job.

- Monica's husband had managed all of the investments during their twenty years of marriage. When they divorced, he suggested that they split the brokerage accounts fifty-fifty. She agreed. Only later did she realize that she had received the part that was difficult to sell and came with a tax bill of $18,000.

- When Helen and Jim divorced, Helen took the $220,000 family home and Jim took the 401(k). The house had a mortgage of $130,000, with monthly payments of $1,700. Because she couldn't make the mortgage payments on her salary, Helen had to put the house up for sale. Forced to sell in a hurry, she lowered the price dramatically to attract buyers. She sold the house for $145,000, and ended up with equity of only $15,000 instead of $90,000.

- One afternoon, during Sharon and Bill's divorce, Bill gallantly offered to take her car to the car wash. Thinking this was the beginning of a reconciliation, she gave him the keys. To her utter surprise, she found out the next day that he had sold the car, which was still in his name, and pocketed the money.

- Connie and Matt retained joint ownership of their small business after their divorce. Once they were no longer romantically attached, he began to squeeze more and more money out of the business. He gave himself a high salary and paid some of his personal expenses from the company accounts. After a few years, he had completely drained the business, and Connie's share was worth nothing.

You can avoid these problems by taking control of the divorce process. By considering the situation ahead of time, and getting professional help in understanding the financial and tax issues facing you, you can avoid being put into a desperate situation. Consider Dixie's reaction to her failing marriage:

Dixie knew that her marriage was going down the tubes. Although it was painful, she decided that she had to accept reality and prepare for the inevitable.

She began by analyzing her financial situation. She gathered financial records on her husband's dental practice to see what his true earnings were. She accumulated records on their assets and debts. She created an estimate of her "post-divorce" expenses to see what life would be like if they ever divorced.

She consulted a divorce financial advisor to determine the likely result of the property division after divorce. The financial advisor used software that showed the long-term financial results of various settlement possibilities. She learned what questions to ask and what to avoid during the divorce.

As Dixie prepared for the future, she set up credit in her own name, stored some cash in a bank account in a nearby city, and put a copy of all important documents into a safe deposit box in her name. She changed the title on her car and took care of needed maintenance for herself and her possessions. She considered child care arrangements and career opportunities for herself after the divorce.

After a few months, Dixie was ready. When her husband cheated on her again for the umpteenth time, she was prepared to make her move. Dixie filed for divorce immediately.

We have written this book so you can take control of your divorce and avoid costly mistakes. Through over 40 years of combined experience with divorcing couples, we have seen people at all ends of the emotional spectrum—scared, resigned, lonely, relieved, confused, joyful, and frustrated—who are looking for real answers to the hard questions they face. We've used our experience and expertise to help thousands of clients get through this difficult ordeal. Like them, we hope you benefit from our cautions and suggestions. We wrote this book to help answer your questions and bring up some important issues you may not have considered.

This book is designed to provide you with the building blocks you need to manage the changes in your life before, during, and after your divorce. We will focus on the "ABCs" of divorce, the basic tools needed to build a solid plan for this stage of your life. Throughout this process, we will emphasize these four attitudes:

## Always Be

- **Careful** – Many mistakes in divorce are made by not thinking carefully about the results of your choices. Be careful and deliberate when making decisions that will affect your future.

- **Cognizant** – Learning as much as possible about the divorce process will make it easier for you to have realistic goals and expectations. Educate yourself and remain cognizant of the financial and legal realities of divorce.

- **Centered** – The "money crazies" of divorce can make it hard for you to focus on what's really important. Try to remain centered on your long-term best interests, not momentary crises and dilemmas.

- **Courageous** – Women, especially, often have a hard time standing up for themselves and getting what they deserve. Take control of the divorce process and be courageous in pursuing what you need and deserve.

A bit of advance planning goes a long way. By preparing yourself for the realities of divorce, you can save yourself a lot of heartbreak—and hassle—in the future. We hope this book will help you protect yourself, provide for your children, and build a bright future after your divorce.

# CHAPTER 1

# Getting Started

---

If you are like most people, divorce will be the largest single financial and legal transaction of your life. You may feel nervous, unprepared, and intimidated. You will face stacks of boring legal documents, frustrating discussions with your ex, and disturbing reminders of married life. We hope this book will help you through this difficult process.

This chapter tells you what to expect during your divorce. We'll discuss the basics of divorce, the legal process, and how you can prepare yourself for the challenges ahead.

## Divorce Basics

A divorce, sometimes called a dissolution of marriage, is the legal process used to terminate a marriage. Although both spouses can file as co-petitioners in some states, only one spouse is required to file for a divorce to occur. The person that files first is called the petitioner or the plaintiff. The spouse who is served is called the respondent or defendant.

Until the 1970s, the only way to obtain a divorce was to prove that the other spouse was guilty of marital misconduct, such as mental cruelty, abandonment, or adultery. Today, all states allow "no-fault" divorce—that is, divorce regardless of who is at fault for the breakup of the marriage. No-fault divorce, as its name implies, is a divorce in which neither party must be proven to have committed any wrongdoing.

No-fault divorces are usually granted for reasons such as incompatibility, irreconcilable differences, or irretrievable breakdown of the marriage. As a practical matter, courts seldom, if ever, inquire as to the nature of the marital problems. The petitioner can simply state that the marriage is no longer working or that the couple has been living apart for a specified period, and a judge will grant the divorce with no questions asked.

## The Divorce Process

Most states require that one of the parties be a legal resident of that state for a certain period of time before a divorce will be granted. Depending on your situation, you may be able to choose the jurisdiction the case will be heard. Talk to an attorney in your locale, or the area in which you anticipate filing your divorce, about the possibilities available to you.

Once you have filed for divorce, your attorney will serve a copy of the summons and complaint on your spouse. If no answer if filed within the time permitted by law in your state (for example, 30 days), you may be granted a divorce by default. Remember, only a judge can grant, or refuse to grant, a divorce. Your spouse cannot "refuse to allow you a divorce." He does not have that power; only the judge does.

The length of time it takes to get divorced varies from state to state. In some states, the divorce can be granted immediately. In other states, there is a cooling-off period, from 30 days to six months.

Discovery is the process of obtaining information, including documents, financial records, and depositions, from your ex. Information about your spouse's checking account, living habits, and retirement plan can all be obtained through discovery.

A temporary order determines what will happen regarding child custody, child support, alimony, living arrangements, and so forth between the time the divorce is filed and the time that it is final. A permanent order is a final order issued by the court, which is binding on both parties and ends the divorce negotiations.

If your spouse contests the divorce, a hearing will be set. However, you don't need to go to court if you and your spouse can agree upon a settlement. Once a settlement is reached, the paperwork is approved by the court and the divorce is final. If you cannot reach an agreement, a court date is set and a judge or other court official will hear the case and decide upon the terms of the final agreement.

Your final divorce decree should include everything that you need to settle the issues of property division, alimony, child support, custody, visitation, and tax issues. This document will affect your life for many years to come, so be sure that it is correct and complete. See Appendix A for a list of items to include in your divorce agreement.

## Legal Separation

Legal separation can be a useful alternative to divorce for certain purposes—for example, to provide health insurance for a spouse who is uninsurable. In addition, some states make divorce faster or easier if there is a prior separation agreement. The law does not require a couple to execute a separation agreement, but it is a wise idea if there are debts, children, support claims or property involved and the parties want to settle these matters in writing before divorcing.

Your separation agreement with your spouse is considered a contract, and you can sue your ex for breach of contract if he violates its terms. If the separation agreement has been made a part of a court order, your ex can also be found in contempt of court if he doesn't follow through.

## If You Are in Danger

If your spouse is physically abusive, seek help right away to protect yourself and your children. First, call your local mental health facility or crisis line for assistance with the legal and psychological aspects of your situation. They will help you navigate the rules for dealing with restraining orders, harassment claims, and the police in your area.

If you are in danger of serious bodily harm, call the police immediately. For further information, call the Domestic Violence Hotline for help at 1-800-333-SAFE (7233) or 1-800-873-6363 for the hearing impaired.

## Prepare Carefully

Making the decision to divorce is a difficult, emotional process. Sometimes you may not be sure that divorce is the right thing to do, yet at other times you may wish it were already over. Once you decide that you are ready to begin, follow these tips to get ready for the divorce.

### Your Finances

* Before you separate, use joint funds to repair your automobile and home, buy clothes for yourself and your children, and other family expenses. Begin your divorce with these expenses already paid, rather than arguing with your spouse about who should pay them later.

* Remember that judges usually enforce the status quo, so start the processes now that you will want to continue after your divorce. For example, go back to school, get braces for the kids, begin medical treatments, etc.

* Cancel all joint credit cards, including charge, department store, and gasoline card accounts. Even if a court rules that you aren't responsible for charges made by your spouse after you separate, the credit card company can hold you responsible while you and your ex sort it out.

* If your spouse moves out and asks the utility companies to cease billing him, they may turn out the lights. Contact the utility companies to be sure they will continue service in your name.

## Legal Matters

- Prepare carefully for your divorce by educating yourself as much as possible. Read a book or take a class on do-it-yourself divorce even if you plan to use an attorney or mediator.

- Learn about the laws of your state. In most community property states (Arizona, California, Idaho, Louisiana, Nevada, New Mexico, Texas, Washington and Wisconsin), marital assets are divided equally between the spouses. In Texas and most other states, the judge can divide the assets in any way that seems fair.

- File for divorce first if your spouse may be moving to another jurisdiction. Many legal aspects of divorce are controlled by local rules. You would be wise to file for divorce first so you can use a local attorney who will be familiar with the rules applicable to your case.

## Your Life in General

- Open a post office box that you can use for your mail before you separate and while you are in the process of divorce. Confidential information can be sent to you there, and it provides a stable mailing address as your life changes.

- Remove sentimental or valuable items to a safe place outside your home. Jewelry, letters, mementos, and keepsakes should be kept at a friend or relative's house, in a safe deposit box, or in rented storage to prevent damage or loss.

- Videotape and inventory household contents. Things have a habit of disappearing in divorce, so keep this information in a safe place for easy access.

- Don't leave home until you have to. Once you move, you may have trouble getting your personal items, and you'll also have difficulty gaining custody of the children you've left behind. And, if you and your spouse both want to keep the house, the resident spouse is more likely to win.

## Gather Information

Don't delay gathering financial information, even if you are not sure you want to divorce. Knowing about your finances will make you a better financial partner if the two of you stay together, and will help you get the best settlement possible if you don't.

Try to obtain copies of all financial records before your divorce begins. Your divorce will cost less if you have the information at hand, rather than gathering it later through formal legal proceedings. Make a clear copy of all tax returns, loan applications, wills, trusts, financial statements, banking information, loan documents, credit card statements, deeds to real property, car registration, insurance inventories, and all insurance policies. Also, copy records that you can use to trace your separate property, such as an inheritance or a gift from your family. These assets will remain yours as long as you can document them.

In addition, find and copy all business tax returns for your spouse's corporation or partnership. The IRS cannot legally give you copies of your spouse's business returns if you did not sign them.

If you can't find any financial statements, make a copy of any loan applications. They generally have the same information and are signed as a true statement of assets and debts.

Write a summary of important facts, including the date you married, your children's birth dates, the date you separated, property brought into the marriage, and other events.

Be sure to document your income and expenses. The more complete your financial records, the less chance your spouse will find transactions to question. Frequent unexplained deposits and cash expenditures will subject your finances to greater scrutiny.

If you and your spouse have a safe deposit box that contains assets, such as cash, jewelry, stock certificates, or important papers, document the contents of the box. Visit the box to photograph and inventory its contents. If possible, invite a witness to go with you who can attest to the inventory. When photographing the contents, place a copy of the day's newspaper in the box to prove that the picture was taken on that date.

Make a detailed list of all of your assets, including retirement plans. Specify the names of financial institutions, their location, account numbers, account names, and balances for easy reference. Remember to list money that people owe to you or your spouse, such as personal loans, security deposits, and utility deposits. Similarly, make a detailed list of all of your debts. Don't forget any unusual obligations, such as lawsuit or installment payments. These debts can be important in later negotiations with your spouse.

If your spouse is unwilling to provide information and you don't have any copies, you may be able to obtain documents directly from the original source. For example, you may obtain copies of your loan application and loan documents from the lending institution. Real estate deeds are on file at the county records office. Your insurance agent can give you copies of your policies. Copies of your bank statements are available directly from your bank for a nominal fee, though retrieving copies of each canceled check is usually prohibitively expensive. If you don't have copies of your personal income tax returns, you may obtain them by filing Form 4506 with the IRS and paying a small fee. You will also be able to obtain copies of business returns directly from the IRS if you signed the copy that was filed. Request that the copies of these forms be sent to your post office box, a friend, or your attorney.

Your spouse may suggest that you don't need the missing financial records and that he is willing to give you generous settlement terms. Remember, now that you and your spouse have separated, you have different economic interests, so be skeptical of any seemingly generous offer. It may be that your spouse feels guilty, so he is driven to give you the lion's share of the marital property. On the other hand, perhaps your spouse is withholding some vital information or trying to smooth talk you into making concessions or giving away important rights. This is more likely to occur if you are reasonably affluent and have a fair number of complicated assets. Before evaluating your spouse's offer, gather all your financial records and enlist the help of an accountant or financial planner trained in divorce issues to help you determine what to do.

Louise had a suspicion that her husband was preparing to divorce her. She had never handled their finances and knew nothing about their financial status. She decided that this was a good time for her to become more knowledgeable.

She began gathering financial records on her investments, debts, income, and expenses. She started sleuthing around her husband's business, a retail store, for financial information.

During the course of her investigation, she discovered that her husband was socking away thousands of dollars in cash, in preparation for the divorce.

By carefully copying the records, she was able to substantiate his actions, and during the divorce negotiations she was able to increase her settlement significantly.

## Cash is King in Divorce

In divorce, everything always costs more and takes longer than you expect. Costs include court filing fees, legal expenses, duplicate living expenses for the spouse who leaves the home, transportation between homes for the children, costs incurred to make yourself feel better—shopping spree, therapy, a good meal out—and a myriad of other drains on your financial resources. Keep in mind that the money previously used to support one household must now stretch to support two. For this reason, you will need to accumulate cash.

If cash is available, set aside some funds to use during the first few months of separation. Otherwise, you may have to borrow or run up costly credit card debt to pay for living expenses.

The cash that you set aside should be safe and readily accessible. Deposit the money into a bank account or money market account in your own name on which you can draw at any time. Don't be tempted to put your cash reserves in time deposit accounts or other accounts that pay a higher interest rate but limit your access to the funds. Remember, the purpose of these funds is to give you cash for use in the difficult and expensive time of divorce—if the money earns some interest, so much the better, but earning interest is not your primary purpose in setting aside the money.

To decide how much cash you need, determine what expenses are likely to come up during the separation and subsequent divorce. This can include security deposits and rental advances, duplicate household furnishings and appliances, attorney retainers, filing fees, and therapy or group counseling costs for you and your children. If you will ultimately receive child support or alimony, you may also need cash reserves while you are waiting for your spouse to send money, or while you are waiting for a court date to set temporary support.

To accumulate the cash that you need, save as much as you can from each paycheck and any other source of income that comes in. Cut back on your expenses where possible in order to stash cash. Unfortunately, those cutbacks in lifestyle may be permanent, as it is nearly impossible to support two households with the same income that supported one household. If you receive extra sums of money, such as a bonus, a tax refund, or income from overtime or an extra job, save as much of that windfall as you can.

Naturally, when it comes time to divide assets, you will have to reveal the cash reserves you have set aside. If you fail to do so, and your ex-spouse later discovers that you had secret bank accounts or other assets, in most states he will be able to open up the divorce case for the purpose of dividing those newly discovered assets, even though you may have spent them long ago.

## Sources of Cash

Here is a list of possible sources of cash during your divorce. Even if you think you may not need them, it might be best to investigate these options just in case.

*   If you have a 401(k) or other retirement plan at work, you might be able to borrow from it. Typically, the loan must be paid back, with interest, within five years.

*   If you have any unwanted items, you might be able to sell them to raise cash. Be sure you both agree to sell the property and that no restraining order bars you from doing so.

*   If you own a home, a home equity loan may be a source of funds. If you qualify, these loans can provide a generous line of credit from which you and your spouse can draw for future expenses, with low required monthly payments. A word of caution: if you plan to keep the house for yourself after the divorce, you will owe the entire balance of the home equity loan because it is a mortgage against the house.

*   If your family or friends are willing to loan you money as you go through this difficult time, you might consider this source of funds. However, before you ask for money that may have strings attached, carefully consider the emotional and interpersonal costs.

*   If you have borrowed money from a bank, credit union, or finance company in the past, you may be able to get a personal loan. The interest on a personal loan might be high, however, so understand the full costs and repayment terms before you borrow.

*   If you have an IRA, consider withdrawing money only as an option of last resort. If you withdraw money from an IRA

before you are age 59-1/2, you will be liable for a 10 percent
penalty along with regular income tax on the money you
withdraw. This can be quite expensive, and will leave you with
far less than you anticipated.

- Of course, credit cards may be a solution, albeit a costly one.
  The interest rate charged on credit cards is generally quite high.
  If your only option is to charge, it's time to radically change
  your lifestyle or you might end up going straight from divorce
  court to bankruptcy court.

---

Olivia's husband walked out on her one day, taking half of their
joint bank and investment accounts—and leaving all of their
joint debt.

Luckily, Olivia had started investigating her financial options
when she suspected that she and her husband might separate. She
had carefully set up credit in her own name, saved some cash in a
separate account, and sounded out family and friends regarding
financial help.

When put in a desperate situation, she put her planning to use
and was able to maintain financial stability until the financial
issues of the divorce were settled.

---

# CHAPTER 2

# Using Divorce Professionals

Whether you decide to handle your divorce mostly by yourself—or through mediation, arbitration, or litigation—you will probably need the services of divorce professionals at some point in the process. In this chapter, you'll discover how to choose the right accountants, attorneys, and financial advisors for your needs. We'll also offer some money-saving tips on how to get the best help for your time and money.

## Explore Your Divorce Options

### Handle Your Own Divorce

In many simple divorces, handling your own divorce is the best option. If you have no children, little property, and an amicable relationship with your spouse, a do-it-yourself divorce may be an excellent choice. Even if your divorce is complex, you don't necessarily need to hire an attorney to take on the whole case. Often, you can gather as much information as possible by yourself, and then hire an attorney by the hour.

However, be careful about getting in over your head. If your situation involves any of the following, you may need to consider a different option.

- You have complicated property issues, such as a family business or farm, bankruptcy, pension plan valuation, stock options, future royalties, disputed titles, or separate property.

- You have children, and are having difficulty coming to an agreement about custody, visitation, or living arrangements.

- You feel confused about your rights or overwhelmed by legal complexities. If you are completely stuck, hiring an attorney for a brief consultation may help you to get back on track—and also help you determine if you need to change course.

- Your spouse files legal papers that contradict your previous agreements, takes unilateral action that threatens you personally or financially, or otherwise acts in an aggressive or dangerous manner.

- You and your spouse are so hostile that you are unable to have rational discussions and can't manage to come to any kind of agreement.

## Use Mediation

Mediation is a divorce alternative in which in which a trained professional, such as a therapist or attorney (and sometimes both), helps you and your spouse to see each other's point of view and arrive at a win-win solution. Typically, mediation takes far less time than traditional litigation, and mediation can be much less expensive and rancorous than turning your divorce over to the court system and dueling lawyers.

Mediators work with both of you together to help resolve your issues. They do not take sides, but rather they help the two of you to reach a workable agreement. Mediation is especially advantageous for couples that will maintain an ongoing relationship after the divorce, such as parents of minor children.

Even if mediation doesn't work for settling the entire divorce, you can use mediation to settle some of the easier issues, which will speed the divorce process and save you money. Of course, you can combine mediation with other legal approaches—that is, work together to settle your issues through mediation, but consult an attorney on your own between mediation sessions to help you clarify your position.

Mediators charge by the session, hour, or day, and are usually paid by both parties. Once your mediation is complete, if the mediator is an attorney he will draft the agreement for you as part of the mediation process. If the mediator is not an attorney, he will draft a memorandum of understanding which summarizes the agreements you reach. You will then use an attorney to draft the agreement in legal form.

---

Maria and Christopher have decided to divorce.

They are unsure if they want to use mediation, which seems very expensive. Mediation would cost about $6,000 for five full days at $150 per hour.

However, a two-day trial with all the preliminaries—discovery, depositions, motions, pre-trial settlement conferences, court reporters, and the rest—would cost at least $25,000 and produce the same or a worse result.

Maria and Christopher decide to try mediation first, and go to court to resolve only the issues on which they can't agree.

---

The following questions will help you evaluate if mediation is appropriate for you. Don't just ask these questions at the beginning of the process. As your emotions, needs, and goals change during the mediation process, re-evaluate these questions and change your approach accordingly.

- Can I stand up for myself?

- Can I avoid feeling intimidated or abused by my ex?

- Do I have as much financial knowledge and power as my ex?

- Does my ex seem committed to being fair?

- Do I feel fairly relaxed and comfortable with the mediation process?

- Can I express my thoughts clearly?

- Can I understand what my ex is trying to express?

- Do I sincerely want to achieve a "win-win" solution?

## Use Collaborative Divorce

We thank Pauline Tesler, J.D., of the International Academy of Collaborative Professionals for providing this information on collaborative divorce.

Collaborative divorce is a team approach to divorce that includes divorce coaches, financial specialists, collaborative law attorneys, and, when needed, child specialists and therapists. Although more professionals are involved in collaborative divorce cases, the cost is lower overall because you receive comprehensive assistance that lessens misunderstandings and disputes after the divorce.

In collaborative divorce, both spouses have specially trained attorneys whose only job is to help them settle the dispute. All participants agree to work together respectfully, honestly, and in good faith to try to find "win-win" solutions. No one may go to court, or even threaten to do so, without terminating the collaborative divorce process.

Collaborative divorce differs from mediation in its comprehensive team approach. In mediation, a single mediator helps the disputing parties settle their case. The mediator cannot give either party legal advice, and cannot help either side advocate its position. In collaborative divorce, each side has quality legal advice and advocacy, as well as a team of other professionals to complete the job.

## Use Arbitration

If your negotiations with your spouse have stalled, you may want to try arbitration as an alternative to full-blown litigation.

Arbitration, also called "rent-a-judge", is useful when most issues have been decided and you are on your way to a final agreement but are still hung up on some critical points such as the value of a business or the amount of alimony.

Both parties go before an arbitrator (often a retired judge from family court) and present their case with or without their respective attorneys. The arbitrator then makes a binding decision regarding the disputed issues. The decision is incorporated into a court judgment and is just as valid as if a judge had decided the issues.

Arbitration is much less expensive than a court battle. You are not bogged down by the costly waits for trial or other court procedures, and the arbitrator is dedicated to your case until it is resolved. Although arbitrators often charge several hundred dollars per hour, you only need to hire one, and issues are often decided quickly.

## Use Traditional Litigation

If all else fails, you can pursue traditional divorce litigation. If your case goes to trial, each of you will need to be present with your respective attorneys, who will charge each of you several hundred dollars per hour. There will be opening arguments, closing arguments, direct examination and cross-examination of witnesses, court reporters, experts, and all of the accoutrements of the law, just as in any other civil case. The whole process will get very expensive, very quickly. Even if you choose the litigation route, try to settle the case as soon as possible to avoid going to court.

## Get Specialized Legal Advice

There are several situations that can make divorce much more complicated. You will need to seek specialized legal advice if you find yourself in any of the following situations.

- **Your spouse is out of the state or country and is unwilling to cooperate.** In this case, you have three potential problems: serving papers on your spouse, discovering your spouse's assets, and getting your share of those assets. It is possible to divorce a missing spouse, but the procedures are slightly different. After filing for divorce, you publish notice of the filing in a local newspaper. If your spouse does not respond to the published notice, a judge may still grant you the divorce. If your spouse has property within the state, the court can generally make orders to satisfy your need for support from that property. Generally, assets can be divided no matter where they located, but the court of your state will have limited control over your spouse or your spouse's assets if they are out of state.

- **Your spouse is mentally ill or incapacitated.** If your spouse is actually mentally ill (not just annoying) and unable to act on his own behalf, a court may need to appoint a guardian or conservator to represent his interests in the divorce case. If you suspect that your spouse is not mentally competent, consult an attorney before filing for divorce. If you don't, any settlement you negotiate with your spouse could be set aside if a court later declares your spouse mentally incompetent.

- **Your spouse dies during divorce.** Even though you may wish that your ex would die, it will make your divorce much more difficult if he does. If he dies before the divorce is final, family court no longer has the right to hear your case and settle the property division issues. Unless he left everything to you in his will or trust, or his property automatically goes to you by joint tenancy, you will probably find yourself in the probate court, doing battle with his heirs.

- **Your spouse is a non-resident alien.** If you are a married to a non-resident alien, US courts cannot award you property or support from property located outside of the country. In addition, the gain on any property you transfer to your spouse in your divorce will be taxable to you. You will need to seek specialized legal advice to get your share of the marital property.

- **One of you is in bankruptcy—or is headed that way.** Money troubles and marriage troubles go hand in hand. If you are having financial difficulty and might be headed for bankruptcy, read the section on bankruptcy in Chapter 8 and consult a bankruptcy attorney.

## Use Financial Professionals

If your divorce involves complicated financial issues, such as separate property, stock options, pension valuation, small business valuation, or career assets, your attorney may need additional financial help from an accountant or financial planner trained in divorce. The financial professional should not only be skilled in the general issues of accounting, taxes, and finance, but also be familiar with issues specific to divorce.

A divorce financial professional, such as a Certified Divorce Specialist, should have a good understanding of forensic accounting (figuring out where the money went), the tax implications of divorce, and the nuances of property division. Network with your attorney, accountant, or financial planner to find someone in your area who is skilled in these matters.

A Certified Divorce Specialist (CDS) has been trained in the specific financial and tax aspects of divorce. They become part of the team with your attorney to provide the financial expertise that is necessary to help you survive financially after divorce. They provide you with personalized charts and graphs that show the financial result of any given settlement proposal.

## Choosing a Divorce Professional

Finding a divorce professional is a lot like finding a good auto mechanic or plumber—the warmer the referral the better. Start by asking your closest friends, then consult with social or business acquaintances, and finally, check with professional societies. Only cold call from the yellow pages as a last resort. Here's where to start looking for an attorney, mediator, arbitrator, or other divorce professional:

- Ask friends who have gone through a divorce for their recommendations.

- Ask your priest, preacher, minister, rabbi, or other religious leader for recommendations.

- Ask other professionals who are helping you with the divorce process, such as accountants, financial planners, or attorneys.

- For attorneys, contact the American Academy of Matrimonial Lawyers, 150 N. Michigan Ave., Suite 2040, Chicago, IL 60601, (312) 263-6477.

- For attorneys, contact the American Bar Association, 750 N. Lakeshore Dr., Chicago, IL 60611, (312) 988-6102.

- For attorneys, visit your local library (or on the Internet at www.martindale.com) and look through the Martindale-Hubbell Directory of Attorneys. This resource has listings of attorneys by city throughout the United States. Read the descriptions and biographies to find attorneys that are Board Certified in domestic relations or family law, and see if he or she is active in organizations for domestic relations attorneys.

- For attorneys, call your State Bar Association and ask for referrals to attorneys in your area. Note: some states now have certified specialists in family law. Ask if your state has such a system and obtain the names of several attorneys in your area.

- For mediators, contact your county family or domestic relations court. If your state requires or authorizes judges to order mediation to resolve child custody disputes, you may be able to get a referral from the court clerk to a private mediator to handle other aspects of your divorce—not just child custody.

- For mediators, contact the Academy of Family Mediators at (781) 674-2663. The Academy provides a national referral service and can send you a list of practitioners in your state.

- For collaborative divorce attorneys, contact the Coalition for Collaborative Divorce at (800) 559-3724.

- For CPAs trained in divorce, contact your state Society of CPAs and ask for a member of the family law specialist section.

- For financial professionals divorce specialists, go to *www.cdsCollege.com* to find a Certified Divorce Specialist (CDS) near you.

- As a last resort, look through the yellow pages.

## How Not to Choose a Divorce Professional

Of course, it's tempting to hire an attorney immediately so you can start to put all of this behind you. However, choosing an attorney is a very important step, that should not be taken lightly. Here are some things not to do:

- **Don't** use your spouse's attorney or an attorney that is a family friend or business associate of your spouse. If you choose someone who may have emotional or financial ties to your spouse or your family, you cannot be sure that you are getting advice that is entirely in your best interest.

- **Don't** use an attorney who is a neighbor, a member of your church, or a business associate if he or she is not a family law attorney. Only family law attorneys have the specialized skills needed to navigate the divorce.

- **Don't** hire the first attorney you encounter. You don't want to make a rash decision on such an important issue.

- **Don't** use the lowest price attorney you can find. An attorney with low hourly rates may make expensive mistakes or end up costing just as much by taking twice as long to prepare documents.

• **Don't** use the highest price attorney you can find. Using an expensive attorney won't guarantee you'll get a better result than if you hire a more reasonably priced attorney.

## Interview Attorneys Carefully

When interviewing attorneys, be sure to find someone who is not threatened by your knowledge and preparation. In fact, seek an attorney who supports your taking an active role. Be sure that your attorney will not undermine your attempts to manage your own affairs.

Discuss fees up front with your attorney. You should know the hourly rate, how portions of hours are billed, and the approximate total cost of the divorce, given the issues you have brought up during the interview.

Choose a knowledgeable attorney. Your attorney should be a specialist who keeps up with the law, is a skilled negotiator, and can communicate with you in plain English. Choose someone you feel comfortable with as well as someone who has a good grasp of the issues of your case.

Interview at least three attorneys, face-to-face if possible. When you meet, ask each attorney the following questions:

• How many divorce cases did you handle last year?

• What portion of your law practice is devoted to divorces?

• Do you consider yourself a litigator, negotiator, arbitrator, or mediator?

• What is your divorce trial experience?

• Will you go to court to litigate this case if it cannot be settled?

• Do you routinely represent clients in my county?

- Will you handle the case yourself, or will an assistant or associate do the work?

- What happens if you get sick or go on vacation?

- What is the procedure for calling you outside of normal business hours if it is necessary?

- How will I be billed?

- How much do you charge for extra expenses (such as postage, faxes, and copying)?

- Do you consider your fees to be below average, average, or above average for this area?

- What can we do to keep costs down?

## Keep Costs Down

Obtain a written fee agreement from your attorney. This agreement will specify how you will be charged and what you can expect from your attorney. Be sure that you read and understand the entire agreement to avoid misunderstandings.

Many attorneys want part or all of their fees in advance, as "insurance" that the fees will be paid. This money is called a retainer. Make sure the retainer is refundable if the attorney doesn't do the work or you fire the attorney before the retainer is exhausted.

The total expected legal fees should be within your budget. If you cannot meet your financial obligations to your attorney as agreed, he or she may discontinue services, leaving you with three options: stop the divorce proceedings, represent yourself, or find another attorney to represent you (paying another retainer to that attorney).

As a general rule, you must retain and pay for your own attorney in a divorce case. However, if you don't have any money, your spouse may be required to pay your attorney's fees. Be sure to ask your attorney about this possibility. If you don't have access to funds because your spouse has handled the money, your attorney may be able to get the court to distribute funds to pay your attorney fees.

Here are some tips for keeping costs down.

- Do some tasks yourself. You can gather documents, file papers, and do anything else that secretaries, paralegals, or law clerks usually do.

- Use your attorney for legal work only. Hire accountants and financial planners who specialize in divorce for complicated financial issues.

- Make sure junior attorneys or paralegals who are familiar with the divorce process and who bill at attorney rates will do only routine tasks. You don't want a new attorney with no divorce experience handling your case and learning divorce law at your expense.

- Read the bill and question your attorney if something doesn't seem right. Catching a simple billing mistake can often save you a bundle.

- Provide photocopies yourself. If your attorney needs to make copies of original documents you provide, you may be charged up to $1 per page!

- Insist that your attorney use regular mail rather than fax or overnight delivery for information you don't need immediately. Postage and other fees incurred by your attorney are passed on to you. A postage stamp costs much less than a $20 overnight delivery.

- Bunch your phone calls. Your attorney may bill in six-minute segments or quarter-hour segments. Either way, you'll find that rather than calling three times and talking four minutes each, you'll save money by bunching your questions and calling just once.

Lynn didn't have a lot of money, but she did have a lot of foresight.

She knew that she couldn't afford to pay an attorney more than a few thousand dollars. Instead of skimping on legal advice, she decided to handle all of the administrative functions herself.

She hired an attorney who let her make copies, file papers, and handle all of the routine tasks of her divorce.

At the end of her divorce, she was financially stable—and she had discovered a new career path: as a paralegal.

# CHAPTER 3

# Navigating the Divorce

Going through divorce can make you feel like the captain of a leaky boat on stormy seas—there seems to be a new crisis at every turn. Sometimes it can help to remember that divorce is not a permanent state—it is a transition period that will one day be completed. Your life will resume its normal course in due time. In this chapter, we'll lay out some ideas that will help you navigate the shoals of the divorce process.

## Take an Active Role

Doing as much as you can by yourself will help you recover more quickly from the divorce because you will have a healthy sense of control over the process, be focused on practical things, and be working with your ex to get things done. Also, taking an active role in the negotiations will help you to reach a better settlement than "letting the attorneys handle it." You will have less conflict and litigation after the divorce, better compliance from your ex, and better sharing of information about the children.

Don't let anyone, including your spouse or a professional you have hired, take control of the divorce process away from you. If you use a mediator, stop the process if your spouse tries to take over, the mediator tries to impose answers on you, or you don't feel the mediator is listening to you. If you are going it alone, don't let your spouse take over and don't assume he will operate in your best interests. If you use an attorney, remember that this is your divorce, not your attorney's. Your attorney may give you advice, but the final decision rests with you.

---

When Ken filed divorce papers after 12 years of marriage, Amanda was devastated.

After a few miserable weeks, she decided to get on with her life and take control of the divorce process.

She made a study of divorce, learning everything she could from professional advisors, friends, and others who had been through divorce. She didn't listen to friends who told her to "let the lawyers handle it." She didn't listen to Ken when he told her that she had to do things his way or he would "leave her and the kids with nothing."

She took care of herself.

After consulting with her attorney and divorce financial advisor, Amanda worked out a plan that was fair to Ken, but provided her with the financial security she needed.

Because she refused to be intimidated by Ken or anyone else, Amanda negotiated a solution that met *her* needs.

---

## Try To Negotiate

Many child-related issues, such as physical custody and specifics about visitation, are best negotiated by you and your spouse. You may also be able to reach general agreements on some or all property issues, such as who will live in the house, whether it will be sold, how retirement assets will be divided, and so forth. Even if your attorney negotiates for you, formulate specific goals for the divorce and make an effort to understand the financial ramifications of your decisions.

As in any negotiation, decide what is most important to you. Identifying the "blue chip" items that are absolute necessities, and the "bargaining chip" items that are not important to you (and the same for your ex), will help you become a better negotiator. Fight for what you need, but let go of what you can live without.

## Be Businesslike

During this trying time, it is quite common to view your attorney as a friend or confidante rather than a paid professional. It is very important to try to keep your relationship businesslike—both for your emotions and your pocketbook. You don't want to waste time discussing non-legal issues at your attorney's hourly rate. Remember, you need an advocate, not a friend. Keep your relationship on a businesslike level by following these suggestions.

- Tell your attorney that you want to hear both the good news and the bad news. You and your attorney must have honest communication in order to work efficiently together.

- When your grief is overwhelming, go home or to a friend's house, not to your attorney. It won't help your financial situation to cry in your attorney's office at $200 an hour.

- Provide all the information that is requested of you, and if you are requesting information from your spouse, make sure you really need it. Withholding information or dragging your feet only increases attorney fees. Requesting unnecessary information just to harass your spouse simply runs up your legal bills.

- Don't obsess about small issues. A divorce settlement that meets your major needs and objectives is sufficient. Don't stall the negotiations and incur substantial legal bills arguing about minor details.

- Watch the clock with your attorney and other professionals. Time is money when you are paying by the hour, so be prepared for each meeting and don't shoot the breeze. You are in your attorney's office to do business.

- Don't declare war. Choose an attorney who can help you solve problems and bring your divorce to a successful conclusion as quickly as possible. A nasty divorce benefits only the attorneys.

- Encourage your spouse to hire skilled counsel. If your spouse receives incompetent advice, he or she may seek an unreasonable settlement.

## Separate Your Emotions from Economics

Because divorce is seen as a breach of the marriage contract, our legal system encourages a battle of the exes to determine who is right and who is wrong. Many divorcing spouses "go for the jugular" and try to prove that their ex is a bad person who deserves to be punished.

When this happens, a simple case—even one where the spouses have a basic understanding of how the issues should be resolved—can quickly turn into a complex case full of suspicion, mistrust, emotional damage, and huge attorney bills. Recovering emotionally from a nasty and expensive divorce is neither easy nor fun.

The more frenzied your emotions, the longer the proceedings and the more costly the divorce. If you can keep your own emotional issues separate from the legal and financial issues of your divorce, you can keep your divorce under control.

While it may be tempting to use money as a weapon, or to be vindictive, that type of emotional behavior will lead to more conflict and only cost you more in the long run.

Here are some strategies to help you to separate emotions from economics:

- Understand all of the steps in divorce process and think about your overall strategy. You don't have to solve all of your problems immediately. It is no better or worse to take a short time or a long time in negotiating a divorce. The key is to avoid a contested divorce. Take your time, and don't let anyone pressure you.

- Insist that all contested issues be mediated or arbitrated. Some attorneys who bill by the hour may advise against this, preferring that you fight it out in court. Just say no and get another attorney.

- Understand each person's role in the process. An attorney is there to advise you on the legal aspects of divorce. A therapist, counselor, or minister helps with the emotional aspects. A financial professional deals with money. Don't use your attorney as your therapist. Similarly, don't decide how to divide a pension or value a partnership interest on the basis of emotions or inadequate advice.

- Take care of yourself. Eat healthy food, get enough rest, and exercise regularly. Don't underestimate the importance of basic personal maintenance to promote a feeling of well being during divorce.

- Avoid isolation. This is the time to rely on old friends and seek out new ones —especially people who are experiencing similar problems. The better you feel, the less likely you are to let your emotions get in the way. If money is tight, check with local support groups or the local mental health department for low cost counseling.

## Keep a Diary

Keep a written log of every divorce-related conversation you have with your attorney, your spouse, and your other advisors. For every conversation, include the date, time started, time ended, who was involved, and a brief synopsis of what was said. A diary serves as a permanent record of the progress of your divorce, and will be very helpful when memories fade. Writing each entry will also help to solidify the conversation in your mind. By doing this you'll avoid wasting time by repeating conversations. If there are disputes over time spent with an attorney or other professional, you'll also have the documentation you need to reduce your bill or have work redone. You may also begin to look forward to how much time and energy will be available for other pursuits after the divorce.

## Manage Your Money During Divorce

After you and your spouse have separated, but before you are divorced, you will need to come to an agreement on how expenses will be paid. Otherwise, you may find yourselves engaged in frequent legal squabbles as bills come due. These conflicts can drain you emotionally, impede progress toward finalizing your divorce, and be expensive as well.

Unless you are both self-supporting, with fairly equal incomes, one of you will probably pay more of the expenses, or will provide funds to the other with which to pay those expenses. In order for the spouse providing the excess funds to receive tax benefit, the payment to the other spouse should be characterized as alimony in a written agreement.

If you own your house, and your property taxes and insurance are not included in your monthly mortgage payment, make sure your temporary order or other agreement specifies who will pay those expenses. Too often future property taxes and insurance premiums are overlooked by judges when making temporary orders. You might find yourself back in court, which is costly, or paying the bill yourself, and trying to get your spouse to reimburse you.

Don't let your spouse starve you out. If you need to spend money for necessities, such as food, clothing, medical care, or expenses for the kids, do so. In most states, money for necessities is considered a joint expense until the divorce is final.

You can also look online for help. The Women's Institute for Financial Education (www.wife.org) is an organization dedicated to helping women become educated on financial matters. Their site can help you learn more about your financial needs during divorce and to connect with other women who are also improving their financial knowledge. Learning about your finances can enhance your feelings of control over your life during this seemingly uncontrollable time.

---

Karen decided that this was as good a time as any to get familiar with finances.

She bought books on personal finance, researched on the internet, and consulted a financial planner.

She knew what to ask for in her temporary support agreement. She created a budget for herself and was able to stay within her means during the divorce.

When the divorce was over, she was able to get right back on track, saving and investing for her future.

---

## Prepare Mentally

Prepare yourself mentally for the worst that can happen. How will you cope if your children get sick, if you have to move in with your parents, if the divorce lasts for years and you lose all of your money? Face the worst so what actually happens will seem easy by comparison.

There is a certain amount of pain intrinsic to divorce. This is normal. Be prepared for this pain, so you can accept it as a necessary response to a huge adjustment, and avoid unnecessary anguish and heartache.

Don't expect your spouse to look out for your interests. Throughout the divorce, your spouse will protect his own interests, which may be quite different than yours. Try to separate emotionally from your spouse.

## Divorce Communication Do's and Don'ts

Communication is extremely important during divorce—and extremely difficult. The most important thing is to maintain as much emotional distance as you can. Tell yourself, "No one can control my mind and my actions," and try to be as logical and honest as possible. The following tips may help:

- Don't let meetings with your ex turn into posturing contests for who's in control or how smart you are. Settling your divorce is the problem you must solve, not a referendum on who was the better spouse.

- Do find common ground and proceed from there. Even if you and your ex can agree only on minor points, it will help build the goodwill to resolve more difficult issues.

- Don't succumb to threats. Money and power are emotionally linked—and allowing your spouse to use money to control you will only leave you powerless.

- Don't give up everything to buy your freedom. Your spouse will still be unhappy, and you'll be equally unhappy when you find yourself impoverished by your foolish gesture.

- Don't make nice to get him back. Even if you hope that you will be able to reconcile, don't bend over backwards to make it happen. Stand up for yourself and get your share. If you reconcile, that's fine, but if you don't, you'll still be able to take care of yourself financially.

- Do pick your battles carefully. Divorce is a series of trade-offs, so be clear about what's important to you. Don't make excessive demands. Control your anger so you can negotiate with a cool head.

- Don't use your kids as bargaining chips. Trading time with the kids for some financial advantage only hurts the kids and rarely results in any financial gain.

## Getting Help

There are many sources of help for divorcing couples to get back on their feet emotionally. Seeking therapy can be an excellent idea. Once you have decided that you are definitely going to divorce, you need a therapist who will help you with this process.

Think of your divorce therapist as a guide to surviving the wilderness of this confusing time. He or she should support you in your choice, encourage your independence, and help you rebuild (or find) your self-esteem. A good therapist can make the process much easier, and keep your friends and family from getting worn out as you go through the stages of grief in recovering from the loss of your marriage.

Communities of other women facing the same issues can also be very helpful. You might consider joining a divorce or transition support group in your area. These groups can be run by a therapist, or just a group of individuals who share similar challenges.

## Top 5 Tips for Women During Divorce

1. Laugh. Don't let the bastards get you down.

2. Treat your friends with kindness. Remember not to abuse their offers of help and encouragement.

3. Stay busy. Throw yourself into your career, your children, your volunteer work, or your hobbies. Do constructive things to take your mind off of insoluble problems.

4. Surround yourself with positive people. Talk to people who make you feel better afterwards, who point out the good side of everything. If you don't know anyone like this, finding new friends might be a good project to keep you busy.

5.  Be assertive. Don't let your ex, your attorney, or your family walk all over you. Try to figure out what is truly in your best interest, and don't let anyone get in your way.

# CHAPTER 4

# Alimony and Maintenance

Alimony is designed to help you get back on your feet again financially after a divorce. It is most often used when one spouse has a high earning ability or the other has stayed home to raise the children. In this chapter, we offer help in understanding the alimony rules, tax considerations, and how best to plan for alimony in your divorce

## Alimony in General

Alimony can be called "spousal support," "maintenance," "rehabilitative maintenance," or simply "alimony, " depending on your state's laws. In most states, alimony is based on each person's needs, earning ability, age, health, the marital standard of living, the length of the marriage and the tax consequences of paying or receiving alimony.

If your marriage was of short duration or you are both in good health and earn fairly equal amounts, it is unlikely you will receive alimony. Also, if you have a prenuptial agreement, that agreement may take precedence over these rules. Check with your attorney if you are in either of these situations.

## Your State's Laws

State laws regarding alimony vary tremendously. In some states, the court can order that alimony be paid for as long as you need it after a long-term marriage. In most states, alimony terminates by law when the recipient dies or remarries. A few states provide that alimony will be decreased if the recipient cohabits with a person of the opposite sex.

Your decree may also specify that alimony will cease on a certain date. Most states will not modify such an agreement, although the state may retain the authority to change such an agreement if the recipient might otherwise go on public assistance. If your decree does not provide for a set termination date, then alimony will continue until further order of the court. The payer may seek a termination any time if he can show that the recipient no longer needs support or that he can no longer pay support. For example, support may decrease if the recipient has become self-supporting through employment or inheritance, or if the payer is unable to pay because of a disability.

If you do not know the rules in your state, you could unintentionally lose your right to alimony. For instance, you and your spouse might negotiate a fixed amount of alimony for a set period. If you designate in your divorce agreement that alimony is non-modifiable, the court will not be able to extend alimony beyond the time specified, even in a long-term marriage.

When alimony is terminated by the court, the court may continue to retain jurisdiction over the issue. This means that if you need support at any time in the future, you can petition the court for an order reinstating alimony.

## Waiving Your Rights

If your divorce decree does not mention alimony, alimony probably can be awarded at a later date if you make a sufficient case for alimony before a judge. If both spouses waive alimony in the decree, then the court will generally deny future requests for alimony.

Do not waive your right to alimony except after close consideration of all of the facts and a thorough discussion with your attorney. Once you waive your right to alimony, you can't get it back.

# Calculating Alimony

## Identify Your Income

The most important factor in computing alimony is the income of both parties. Correctly identifying all income received by both spouses, both taxable and non-taxable, is very important.

Start with the total income from your federal income tax return. Then add any non-taxable income, such as interest on municipal bonds and contributions to retirement plans. Also look in your check register for any deposits that might point to additional sources of income.

Net income from a business is computed differently for alimony purposes. For instance, depreciation, while deductible for tax purposes, likely will not be deducted from net income for alimony purposes. Similarly, some home office deductions are disallowed for alimony purposes because they would still be necessary living expenses if the business did not exist. Business travel and entertainment may have a personal component that will be added back to income for alimony purposes, as will personal automobile expenses. If you will receive alimony, it is in your best interest to investigate these issues. Ask your financial professional or accountant to help you through the process.

## Document Your Expenses

Use a budgeting form, spreadsheet, or personal finance software to create a list of past expenses and a budget for your future needs. Keep receipts, cancelled checks, and other documentation so that you can back up your claims in court. By carefully documenting living expenses, you may be able to justify an increased alimony payment.

# Alimony Taxation

## The Five "D" Test

In general, alimony is taxable income to the person receiving it and a tax deduction for the person paying it, but only if it passes the "Five D" test. To be deductible by the payer (and taxable to the recipient), it must be paid in DOLLARS, under a DECREE or written agreement, and cease on the recipient's DEATH. After the divorce you must maintain your DISTANCE (can't live with your ex), and the payments can't be DESIGNATED as non-taxable alimony or child support. If the payments you receive do not meet all of these tests, they are not taxable to you as alimony. They are non-taxable gifts from your ex.

## Making Payments for Your Spouse

Payments made on an asset that you still own are not considered alimony. For example, if you own a home in which your spouse resides, and you make the mortgage payments on the house, that payment won't qualify as alimony because you are making the payment on an asset you still own. (However, you may be able to claim the interest as a deduction on your tax return as interest paid on a second residence). On the other hand, if you make the car payment on a car owned by your ex, the payment *will* qualify as deductible alimony, if it is called for in your support agreement, because you are making the payments on behalf of your spouse for an asset that is not yours.

## Alimony Recapture

Alimony recapture provisions were enacted to prevent couples from disguising otherwise non-deductible property settlement payments as deductible alimony. If you make alimony payments that will drop more than $15,000 annually during the first three years after your divorce, you may be subject to alimony recapture.

You could run afoul of the alimony recapture rules if your ex agrees to pay your attorney's fees, but wants the payment to be described as additional alimony so that he can deduct the payment on his tax return.

Bert offers to mow Amy's large yard every week, which he claims has a value of $600 per month. He wants to consider that his alimony payment. This is not deductible because alimony has to be in **dollars**, not services.

Amy loses her job and finds another position that will start in six months. She asks Bert for extra financial help for a while. Bert sends her an extra $500 a month, but he cannot deduct it as alimony because it is not stated in their **decree**.

If the decree says payments will continue after Amy dies, the alimony will not be considered deductible because it is payable after her **death**.

Bert and Amy live in a huge house. After their divorce Bert resides in the left wing and Amy resides in the right wing. Even if they never see or speak to one another, any alimony paid is not deductible, because they continue to reside in the same house, so they haven't maintained **distance** after the divorce.

Bert has lots of tax deductions from his business, and Amy is in a fairly high tax bracket. Bert and Amy therefore decide to **designate** the alimony as non-deductible to Bert, which will make it non-taxable to Amy. They also could have designated it to be child support, which is non-deductible to Bert and non-taxable to Amy, and accomplished the same result.

If the payment exceeds $15,000, he may be subject to recapture provisions. Consult a financial advisor before your divorce agreement is finalized to avoid this tax trap.

## Consider Family Support

Child support is not taxable to the recipient or deductible by the payer. If the payer is in a higher tax bracket than the recipient, it may make sense to call all of your payments undifferentiated family support

> If Bob pays Caroline $50,000 in alimony in the first year,
> $30,000 in the second year, and $10,000 in the third year, Bob
> would be subject to the recapture provisions at the end of the
> third year. Using a complex formula, Bob would be liable for
> taxes on $22,500 of alimony recapture. He would have to report
> $22,500 of additional income on his income tax return, and
> Caroline would receive a corresponding deduction on her tax
> return.
>
> This is so even if the reductions in the second or third year were
> not part of the divorce decree. If the decree called for $50,000
> alimony every year, but Bob became delinquent and thus made
> the lower payments, the alimony recapture rules would still come
> into play.
>
> Similarly, if Bob and Caroline renegotiated their settlement or the
> court changed their agreement in the second or third year, the
> alimony recapture rules would still take effect. The only
> exceptions to the rules are if either Bob or Caroline dies or
> Caroline remarries.

instead of alimony. This way, the entire payment becomes deductible by the higher-earning taxpayer, and is taxed at the lower tax rate of the recipient, resulting in less tax paid to the government.

The exception to this rule is if your divorce decree provides that alimony or family support will decrease or terminate upon an event relating to a child, such as the child reaching a certain age, marrying, dying, leaving school, becoming employed, or moving out. In this case, the amount of the reduction in alimony will be treated as child support. It is not legal to deduct it as alimony, regardless of what is specified in the divorce decree.

Similarly, if the alimony is to decrease on a certain date, and that date is within six months before or after your child reaches the age of majority in your state (18 or 21), that decrease is considered disguised child support and cannot be deducted by the payer. The rules are somewhat more complex and equally as strict if the decree calls for two or more reductions because of several minor children. As you can see, the rules for the deductibility of family support are very complicated, so consult a financial advisor if you are considering this option.

---

Janis and David are divorcing.

Their son will live with Janis until he graduates from high school in six years. They agree that David will pay alimony of $3,000 per month for six years and then drop it to $2,000 per month for four more years, after their son leaves home.

Because their agreement provides that alimony will drop from $3,000 to $2,000 when the child reaches majority, this is a reduction based on an event related to a child, and part of the alimony is disallowed as a tax deduction.

Because of this provision in their divorce agreement, David would only be entitled to deduct $2,000 of the alimony paid each year. The $1,000 decrease would be considered disguised child support, which is not deductible. Janis will pay tax on only $2,000 of the $3,000 she receives.

---

## Consider Lump-Sum Support

Consider receiving your alimony as a lump sum payment instead of monthly checks. Payers default on monthly alimony payments about 50 percent of the time. A smaller lump sum that you actually receive is better than monthly payments that never arrive. To avoid alimony recapture rules that we discussed earlier, it is best to designate this payment as non-taxable support, which we explain in greater detail in the following section. Another option would be to designate the amount due as property settlement, which is also non-taxable. But be careful:

it is often easier to enforce a provision for payment of alimony, and in addition, an obligation to pay alimony survives bankruptcy. So if he fails to pay you, you'll be better off if your agreement called the amount non-taxable support rather than non-taxable property division.

## Consider Non-taxable Support

While alimony is generally taxable to the person receiving it and deductible by the person paying it, you have another option. Alimony that would ordinarily be taxable to the recipient and deductible by the payer can be made non-taxable and non-deductible by simply stating so in your divorce decree or in separate agreement. The spouse receiving the support must attach the written statement to her income tax return.

If the after-divorce tax bracket of the payer is lower than the after-divorce tax bracket of the recipient, it may be to your advantage to make alimony non-taxable. Although this is an unusual situation, it might be occur if the payer has many tax deductions, credits, or loss carryovers. Consult a tax advisor to determine which strategy would yield you the greater overall tax savings.

Usually, the decision about taxability of alimony is made at the time of divorce. You can, however, specify in your divorce decree that you will make the decision annually. Your divorce decree would state that your alimony will follow the traditional rules of being taxable to the recipient and deductible by the payer unless both of you specify in writing that treatment for a particular year will be different. Consider this kind of option if one or both of you expect your incomes and deductions to fluctuate year to year and there is a high degree of cooperation between you and your ex.

## Getting Paid

## Request a Wage Assignment

If your spouse is employed (but not self-employed), you can request that the support be withheld from his wages and remitted to you each month. A wage withholding order is the easiest and most effective way to assure that alimony payments will be made on time, and many states now provide for an automatic wage withhold, unless it is waived by both parties.

## If He Doesn't Pay

After the divorce is final and you go your separate ways, you will still maintain a financial connection based on alimony. If your former spouse does not make payments on time, or your agreement permits future modifications, you may find yourself back in court once again.

If the alimony becomes past due, you can take legal action to garnish his income—that is, to have a portion of his earnings or other funds seized and remitted to you. Once the court issues a writ of continuing garnishment, it can be served upon anyone who holds funds for the payer, including employers, banks, and investment companies.

If your spouse is behind in his payments, you can try to obtain a court judgment for the amounts past due, called "arrearages." Once you have a judgment, you can record a lien on property, which will prevent it from being sold unless you are paid, or a levy on bank accounts, which will allow you to receive whatever funds are in the account that day.

You can also seek contempt charges against your ex. However, it is unlikely that your ex will actually go to jail. Of course, if he does, being in jail will make it difficult for him to earn the money to pay the alimony!

## Modifying Alimony

## Two Types of Alimony

There are two types of alimony: open-ended and non-modifiable. Openended alimony can be increased, decreased, or stopped as circumstances change. If your decree says that alimony is to be paid until further order of the court, either of you may seek modification based on changed circumstances. For example, if you are the payer and have lost your job or retired, or the recipient has obtained a job or promotion, you can request a reduction.

Non-modifiable alimony is paid for exactly as long as is stated—no less, no more. If your decree states a set amount of non-modifiable alimony, then a court can't modify the amount.

---

Scott was to pay open-ended alimony to Chelsea for six years. If Chelsea got married in two years, maintenance would stop. If Chelsea became disabled before the end of the six years and needed alimony to continue for a longer period of time, she could petition the court to increase the length of the alimony. If Scott lost his job and couldn't pay alimony, he could petition the court to review their case and lower or cease his alimony payments to Chelsea.

Fred and Susan agreed that Fred would pay non-modifiable maintenance to Susan for six years. Even if Susan re-married in two years, her maintenance would still continue for the full six years. If Fred lost his job, he still would have to continue to make the same maintenance payments. If Susan became disabled, she would not be able to get maintenance for a longer period of time than they had agreed.

---

## When to Modify Alimony

Alimony increases are based on your needs and your lifestyle before the marriage, not on your ex's future earnings. If you receive support and your ex-spouse gets a large raise or inheritance after your divorce, most judges will deny your request for an alimony increase for two reasons:

- You have not demonstrated that *your* needs have changed, and

- Alimony is generally limited to the lifestyle enjoyed by the couple during marriage.

If you pay alimony and become unable to make the payments called for in your divorce decree, seek modification of support immediately. Because courts rarely grant retroactive modifications, your ex-spouse can seek enforcement of the past due alimony. Inability to pay cannot be used as a defense.

## Funding Your IRA with Alimony

You don't need to have a job to save for your retirement. Even if you don't have income from a job or business, you still can fund an IRA for the greater of the amount of your alimony or $3,000 per year (for 2002 through 2004). If your are covered under an employer retirement plan, your modified adjusted gross income must be under $40,000 a year in order to qualify for a fully deductible IRA.

# CHAPTER 5

# Child Support

When a marriage ends, you cease being husband and wife, but your roles as parents continue if you have children. Issues regarding children often touch deep nerves, and child support can be a source of contention in many divorces. Your needs and your ex's needs may clash, causing difficult emotions that can cloud the basic process of determining and continuing support. In this section, we'll try to take the sting out of the whole issue by explaining the process of determining support, what you can expect in court, and how to follow up once support has been awarded.

## Understanding Child Support

### Child Support Guidelines

Child support guidelines vary from state to state. Although most states rely on two primary factors to determine child support—the parent's ability to pay and the children's needs—the calculation of these items can differ quite a bit.

Some states consider the net income of only the non-custodial parent, but most consider the net income of both parents. Some states consider the amount of time the child spends with each parent, while others only consider who has custody. Most states require that the formula consider support paid for children from any other relationship and child care expenses the custodial parent incurs to work or attend school, but some states do not.

A few states take business or personal educational expenses, catastrophic losses, heavy debts, or other pressing cash needs into account. Other states do not permit a reduction for these items, favoring the payment of child support before considering any financial hardships.

Courts generally have the power to order additional support if the child has extraordinary expenses relating to education or health care. A few states increase child support to cover children's extracurricular activities. In contrast, many states permit a lower child support award than what's required under the formula if *both* parents agree to it and the child will be adequately supported.

Child support usually ends at age 18 or 19, although a separation or divorce agreement may set a different age, such as upon graduation from college or at age 21. If the child is disabled or handicapped, the court may order child support to continue for the child's entire life.

## Calculating Child Support

To compute the amount required by your state, you will need a copy of your state's formula. Call your local court to see if there is a copy available at the clerk's office. If not, obtain a copy from a divorce paralegal, divorce support group, or family law attorney.

Fighting over child support in court rarely happens because most judges simply apply the state's formula. In general, the only exceptions to the rules are when:

• The non-custodial parent's income is extraordinarily high

• The non-custodial parent would be unable to live on the amount that remain after the child support payment

• Either parent has remarried or has a live-in mate.

To calculate child support, plug both parents' income and expenses into the formula. Don't forget to include any unusual needs that might be allowable in your state, such as orthodontic work, after-school tutors, vacations, sports, lessons, summer camp, or therapy. Make sure that your settlement agreement specifies which additional expenses will be included in your child support formula.

## Other Financial Matters

In addition to child support, you and your ex should negotiate other financial matters relating to your children. Consider the following questions:

- Who will maintain health insurance for the children?

- Who will pay for non-covered medical expenses and deductibles?

- Who will pay for counseling or other therapy for the children?

- Who will pay for school expenses, such as sports equipment, activity fees, and group trips?

- How will college and higher education costs be paid?

- If one of you dies, how will your minor children's expenses be met?

## Consider a COLA

Consider including a cost of living adjustment (COLA) clause in your settlement agreement so that you don't have to go back to court as inflation decreases the buying power of your original child support settlement.

If your spouse is reluctant to include a COLA clause in your settlement agreement, remind him of the advantages to him for including such an agreement. By including such a clause, he will be reducing the odds that he will be dragged back into court with a request for an increase of child support, saving a great deal of money and aggravation.

In addition, a COLA clause in the divorce decree will ensure that he will be meeting the children's financial needs as they grow. Agreeing to an automatic cost of living increase will not lock him into future payments he cannot afford. If his circumstances change and he cannot afford the amount he has been paying—for example, he loses his job or becomes disabled—he can then petition the court for a decrease.

If your ex refuses to include a COLA, all is not lost. In some states, you can petition for an automatic increase in a very easy process that doesn't even require an attorney.

---

April and Dan had two children, ages 2 and 4, when they divorced.

No matter what April said, Dan refused to include a COLA clause in their divorce agreement.

As the children grew up, their needs increased, and April was having trouble making ends meet.

She contacted her ex and told him how much it cost to raise the children. He said, "So sue me."

So she did.

After being served with a court date, Dan reluctantly agreed to increase child support to the amount from the child support formula, calculated using his current income and the children's current expenses, not the income and expenses at the time of their divorce.

---

## Include Late Fees

If you receive support, try to include a clause in your divorce agreement that makes your ex-spouse liable for a late fee if he is delinquent in his payment of child support. This may motivate him to make timely payments instead of letting them slide.

Your ex may resist a late fee clause. However, it is also to his advantage not to fall behind in support payments, as he won't want to pay legal costs (when he is hauled into court for failure to pay support) on top of accumulated arrears. Tell your ex, "If you don't intend to fall behind in child support, then it shouldn't matter to you whether or not the agreement calls for late fees—you'll never have to pay them!"

## After the Divorce

### Keep a Calendar

Keeping a calendar of the days (and nights) your child spends at your house and your ex-spouse's house is important for two reasons.

First, if your state includes in the computation of child support the percentage of time the child spends with each parent, a calendar will show indisputably when the child was where. This may help you negotiate the initial amount of child support and also subsequent modifications.

Second, a calendar will be helpful if the IRS requires you to prove your right to claim head of household filing status.

### Don't Interfere with Visitation

If your ex is late in paying his obligations, don't interfere with visitation rights or criticize him to your children, family, or friends. The more connection a non-custodial parent feels with his children, the more likely he is to pay child support on a regular and continuing basis. Undermining his relationships with the children will only undermine his motivation to pay the support. Although it is sometimes difficult to do, don't let money issues impact your children's relationship with their father.

In addition, courts consider child support and visitation separate issues. Regardless of his payment status, interfering with visitation can get you into big trouble. If you interfere with his right to visitation, you could be held in contempt of court, fined, and have to pay his attorney fees to boot. If you go so far as to kidnap the children or conceal them from your ex-spouse, you may lose custody.

Of course, if your ex is abusive, addicted to drugs, or otherwise dangerous to your children's well being, you should take immediate action. Petition the court to allow only supervised visitation in the presence of a third party or to deny visitation altogether.

## Show Me the Money

Child support is a very serious obligation. Non-payment can have serious financial consequences that will affect his finances for a very long time. In most states, you can collect delinquent child support until your child reaches 18 or 21. Many states also allow the custodial parent or state collection unit to collect delinquent child support for a several years after the child reaches the age of majority. The court can add all reasonable costs incurred in collecting the support, often including attorney fees. In addition, many states provide for interest—and even penalties—on delinquent payments.

If your ex disappears while owing child support, you can file a declaration to that effect with the court. The child support enforcement unit can make a parent locator search using federal and state agency information and will notify the court of his last known address and employer. Parent locator services generally have access to state utility connection records, motor vehicle records, and tax and property records. If a statewide search is not fruitful, the court can refer the case to a federal parent locator service, which can search records at the Department of Health and Human Services, Social Security Administration, Internal Revenue Service, and Department of Defense.

In some states, if he is chronically delinquent in paying child support, he may be ordered by the court to deposit one year's child support payments into an account to secure future support payments, or to post a bond to secure payment.

There are further consequences to non-payment of support. In many states, he can be denied a business license or driver's license or even have a professional license revoked if he doesn't pay child support. Also, arrears in excess of $1,000 will be reported to credit bureaus, affecting his ability to obtain a mortgage, car loan, credit card, or other loans for many years.

All states have laws authorizing judges to order that child support be paid through some form of automatic wage attachment, often called wage assignment or wage withholding. The wage withholding requires the employer to deduct from the employee's wages enough money to cover the monthly child support, and to send that money directly to you at the end of the month.

However, wage withholding does have some limitations. If your ex loses his job, the wage withholding order will be ineffective. If he is self-employed, wage withholding is not possible. If he is employed in another state, the process of obtaining a wage withholding order is much more cumbersome.

When wage withholding isn't available or isn't enough, here are two other methods to investigate:

- Contact your local child support enforcement unit, which can be a part of the district attorney or state attorney's office. The unit can receive and disburse support payments and act as a prosecutor in the enforcement process. They will first try to use persuasion to have your ex comply with the support obligations. If that fails, they may sue your ex. They can also have your ex's income tax refunds intercepted, as well as collect a portion of disability benefits, and workers' compensation. In some states, the unit also can tap into public and private employer pensions and lottery winnings.

- Sue your ex and obtain judgment for the past due child support. You can then record a lien against any real property he owns.

Once you have a judgment, the court can appoint a receiver to
preserve property that can be used in the future to satisfy child
support obligations. You can contact a sheriff or marshal to levy
bank and investment accounts. If your ex is self-employed, the
sheriff or marshal can stand at the cash register or reception
desk and collect receipts from customers as they come in.

---

After the divorce, Cathy's ex took off for parts unknown.

He didn't visit their two children, ages 5 and 7, and he certainly
didn't pay any support.

Cathy contacted the local child support enforcement unit.
Unfortunately, they were unable to find him.

Though disappointed, Cathy did not give up.

Each year, she would contact them to update their search. Several
years after the divorce, she discovered that her ex had inherited
some real property from his grandmother.

Cathy was able to put a lien on the property. When her ex sold it
to raise cash, she received all of her back child support, attorney
fees, and collection costs.

---

## When to Modify Support

If there has been a substantial change in circumstances, due to inflation, increased living expenses, or a change in the earnings of the other
parent, you can seek a modification of support.

Chances are good that you or your ex-spouse will seek a modification
of child support sometime before your children are grown. That is
because changing circumstances can wreak havoc on the most carefully
negotiated child support arrangement. If one of you loses your job, has

a reduction in hours worked, or becomes injured or disabled, a support payment that once seemed fair will rapidly become unreasonable.

Child support orders cannot be modified retroactively. If you find your child support inadequate to pay the bills, go to court immediately for an adjustment. The sooner you start the process, the better off your finances will be. In order to modify child support, you usually must show a change in circumstances since the previous order. Changes that qualify include:

- An increase or decrease in the income received by either parent—including an increase in income from a new job or raise, or loss of income due to unemployment, disability or retirement

- New needs of the children—including expenses for tutoring, counseling expenses, participation in sports, private school, music lessons, or medical problems

- New child sharing arrangements—for instance, the child moves in with the noncustodial parent or a relative or a friend, the parents share custody or the percentage of time the child spends with each parent changes (if that is considered in your state)

- New child support laws—in most states, a change in the child support law provides an opportunity to modify child support payments.

## How to Modify Support

If circumstances have changed such that you need to seek a modification, you do not necessarily have to argue in court to get one. Compute the amount of the modification you need, then present your request to your ex-spouse and ask for the change. If you can reach an accord, you can write up an agreement and present it to the judge for a signature.

The judge will review the amount in your agreement by calculating support using the state's guidelines. If the amount you have agreed upon deviates from the amount required by state law, the court may ask you both to explain why.

If the agreed upon amount is above the guideline, the court will probably ask the payer if he can truly afford that amount. If the agreed upon amount is below the guideline, the court might ask you to include a statement in your agreement that the children do not receive public assistance and are not likely to receive public assistance in the future. If you cannot reach an agreement, the parent who needs the modification will have to decide if the modification is worth the financial and emotional hassles of fighting each other in court. The parent opposing the modification also must decide whether it is more cost-effective to fight the modification in court or to try to find a middle ground and avoid an expensive legal battle.

If you're arguing over an amount in excess of the formula, the judge may lose patience with the parent who doesn't want to share his wealth with his children. Conversely, the courts do not look favorably on a custodial parent who demands too much and refuses to recognize the realities of the non-custodial parent's other obligations. You will both need to collaborate to create a workable support agreement.

# CHAPTER 6

# Property Division

Before you begin to negotiate your divorce settlement, you must know what you own and what you owe together—and what is your property alone. In addition to considering the easily identifiable assets like your home and cars, this chapter will discuss financial assets, such as retirement plans, and intangible assets, such as future income.

## Marital Property and Separate Property

If assets were acquired with income you received during the marriage, they are considered marital property and are part of what is called the marital estate—the property that will be divided during divorce. Separate property is

- What you brought into the marriage

- What you inherited during the marriage

- What you received during the marriage as a gift.

In most states, money you brought into the marriage, gifts, inheritances and payments for personal injuries are your separate property, if you can trace them to assets you now own. Assets bought with money you brought into the marriage or with income generated from property brought into the marriage, may be considered your separate or marital property, depending on your state's laws.

Sometimes, the property you and your spouse are dividing has both separate property and marital property components. This may be the case, for example, if you used an inheritance (separate property) as a down payment on a house and then used income from your job (marital property) to make the mortgage payments.

Some examples may help to clarify these concepts.

### Separate property, Take 1:

Caroline is married to Steven. Caroline's wealthy sister gives her a gift of $10,000, made out to her alone. She puts the check into a savings account in her name only. This money is her separate property.

Caroline moves the money from the savings account to a certificate of deposit in her name only, and then when the certificate matures she redeposits the money into savings. The funds are still her separate property.

As long as she keeps those funds separate, then they will be considered her separate property.

The interest that her funds earn in the savings account or certificate of deposit may be her separate property or may be considered marital property, depending on her state's laws.

## Separate Property, Take 2:

Michelle's great-uncle left her $30,000 in cash. She put the money into an account in her name alone. This is her separate property.

Michelle marries Dan. She uses her inheritance money to make a down payment on a house, in her name alone. The house is her separate property.

Michelle and Dan begin making payments on the mortgage from their joint checking account. In some states, the inheritance she received is now part of a marital asset, the house. However, in other states, the house is still her separate property, though a portion may be marital property due to the mortgage payments made during marriage.

Michelle and Dan sell the house and Michelle puts the money back into a savings account in her name alone. In some states, the money would be considered her separate property. In other states, it would be considered marital property because it has been commingled with marital property in the form of the house.

## Separate Property, Take 3:

As a single career woman, Denise buys a lovely condo, which is her separate property.

When she marries Don, she adds his name to the deed in a fit of passion. The house is considered marital property.

In some states, she would be allowed to recoup her equity in the house at the time she changed the deed, but in other states the equity would be considered a gift to the marriage and the entire value of the equity would be considered marital property.

## Separate property, Take 4:

Stan bought Sheryl a beautiful diamond necklace three years ago. Unfortunately, the necklace lasted much longer than their marriage.

If the necklace is considered a gift, it is Sheryl's separate property. However, if Stan can prove that it was bought as an investment, in some states it is considered marital property.

# Property Division Considerations

## Consider Separation Dates

Depending on the state in which you live, the date of separation can have a profound impact on your share of the property. In some states, property received after you physically separate is not considered marital property. If you know your spouse is about to receive a large bonus or pension plan contribution, you may not want to move out until it has been received. Of course, if you are the one about to receive the money, you may want to separate before it is received in order to keep it for yourself.

In other states, property received until the time the spouses sign a separation agreement or file the first divorce papers with the court is considered marital property. In this case, you may be able to physically separate yourself but not lose out on your share of the newfound marital property. If you're about to receive a great deal of money, you might want to move quickly to prepare a separation agreement or to file the papers with the court before the money is received.

In some states, marital property continues to accrue until the date the divorce is final, so the timing of the divorce is not as crucial to your financial picture.

## Consider Liquidity

Liquid assets are cash or easily converted to cash. Illiquid assets, such as real estate, collections, and businesses, are not easily converted to cash. Be sure that you will have enough liquid assets to keep you afloat during and after the divorce.

## Consider Hidden Assets

Your spouse may have colluded with an employer to delay bonuses or raises, arranged a false debt repayment to a friend, or paid a salary from the business to a non-existent employee. If you suspect that your spouse is hiding information from you, copy as much financial information as you can. This includes bank statements, cancelled checks and checkbooks, savings account passbooks, income tax returns (both personal and business), gift tax returns, financial reports, applications for loans, and financial statements from the business. If your spouse is playing financial games, you will need those documents to reveal his actions to the judge.

Conversely, don't try to hide assets yourself. You'll likely be found out and incur the wrath of both your ex and the judge. Your divorce will be more straightforward and less expensive if you tell the truth and reveal all of your assets.

## Consider Using Property Settlement Notes

When all else fails, a property settlement note can be an excellent way to move stalled divorce negotiations forward. A property settlement note is used when there are insufficient assets or cash for one party to buy out the other party's interest in an asset. For example, you could take the house and pay your spouse for his share of the equity with a property settlement note.

The note should provide for payments of principal and interest at a reasonable rate. You and your ex decide on the number of years, the interest rate, and the monthly amount to be paid. The principal is not taxable to the recipient or deductible to the payer, as it is considered a division of property. The interest, however, does have to be declared as taxable income.

Property settlement notes can be dangerous. They must be properly drafted and collateralized so that they are enforceable and survive bankruptcy (see Chapter 8).

Sylvia and Bert are getting divorced. Sylvia wants to keep the house, which has equity of $170,000.

Bert's business is appraised at $350,000. These are their only two assets.

To divide their property equally, Bert needs to pay Sylvia $90,000. Since Bert doesn't have $90,000 in cash, Sylvia can accept a property settlement note that pays her $1,065 per month for 10 years.

Sylvia should have her attorney carefully draft a note secured by his business property.

## Tax Considerations

Knowing the tax basis of an asset is important during divorce. The higher the tax basis relative to the item's current value, the lower the gain and the taxes owed on that gain when you sell it. If you must choose between two assets of similar value during the divorce, take the one with the higher tax basis so that your future income tax bill (when you sell) will be lower.

For this reason, money in retirement accounts generally is worth less than money in bank accounts, since retirement money will be taxable when withdrawn. Reduce the value of such accounts by the taxes you eventually will pay to see if you are receiving a fair share. Ditto highly appreciated assets or depreciated rental property that will have large taxable gains when sold.

Here's how to find the tax basis of common assets:

## *Your Home*

- Check the closing statement from the time of purchase for total price paid, plus other costs paid at closing that add to your basis.

- Add any remodeling or improvement costs. Improvement costs are those that add to the value of the home, prolong its useful life, or adapt it to new purposes, such as adding a bathroom, putting in new plumbing, or paving the driveway. Don't include the cost of repairs that simply maintain but don't improve the property. Repairs include painting, fixing floors, repairing roof leaks, and replacing broken windows.

- Deduct any untaxed gain from the sale of houses in the past. Under tax rules in effect until 1997, you could defer gain on the sale of your house by buying a replacement residence. If you have deferred gains (you made a profit, but didn't pay taxes on the profit at that time) on the sale of homes in the past, the tax basis of your residence will be reduced by the untaxed gains on all of the previous houses you've owned.

## *Stocks, Bonds, and Mutual Funds*

- Check the total amount paid on the statement for the month you purchased the investment, or on your purchase confirmation. This will include any commissions you paid.

- Add any dividends you have reinvested.

## *Rental Property*

- Check the closing statement for total price paid, plus other costs paid at closing.

- Add any remodeling or improvement costs, using the same rule as for your primary residence.

- Subtract any depreciation you've deducted on previous tax returns.

## Tax Basis, Take 1:

Sophie, age 38, and Drew, age 39, had two assets: a savings account worth $35,000 and an IRA worth $35,000.

When they divorced, they decided that Drew would take the savings account and Sophie would take the IRA.

Did Sophie get a good deal?

If Drew decided to take all the money out of the savings account, he would get $35,000, and no taxes would be due. However, if Sophie decided to take all the money out of the IRA, she would owe approximately $13,300 in Federal and state taxes plus $3,500 in penalties, leaving her with $18,200. Sophie has actually received far less than half of the marital assets.

## Tax Basis, Take 2:

Ricky and Lucy own 1,000 shares in XYZ no-load mutual fund and also purchase 1,000 shares in ABC no-load mutual fund. Both are worth $15 per share, or $15,000.

Lucy may think it doesn't matter how the funds are divided—but she should. They bought ABC shares eight years ago at $5 per share and XYZ shares five years ago at $10 per share. Although both funds are now worth $15,000, each funds' taxable gain when sold is very different.

On ABC, it is $10,000 ($15,000 minus the $5,000 originally paid). On XYZ, it is only $5,000 ($15,000 minus the $10,0000 originally paid). If Lucy takes the ABC fund, she will owe much more in taxes when she sells than Ricky will when he sells the XYZ shares.

# Your Home

Your home is often the largest marital asset. It is also the most difficult to divide. You have three choices to divide the home: keep it, sell it, or continue joint ownership.

## Keeping the House

Make sure you can afford the costs associated with your house if you want to keep it. Be sure to consider the cost of maintenance, repairs, homeowner's association fees, gardeners, and other household expenses. Although you may be able to afford the mortgage, the other expenses may break your budget.

You can exclude up to $250,000 of capital gain when you sell your primary residence if you've lived there for two of the five years before sale. The tax basis and the sales price will determine the capital gain on the sale. Basis is generally the cost of the house and is not related to the remaining balance of the mortgage. The basis may be affected by improvements, sales costs, and sales of previous homes. You may want to have an accountant or financial professional verify the basis before you agree on your settlement.

## Selling the House

If you and your spouse sell the house while you are both owners, you will share the costs of sale, and you can exclude up to $500,000 of gain. If, on the other hand, you become the sole owner of the house in the divorce settlement, when you sell it, the entire cost of sale and capital gains liability will be yours alone. If the gain exceeds $250,000 you will have to pay tax on the excess over that amount.

## Joint Ownership

Some couples agree to continue jointly owning the home after the divorce until a specified future time—for example, when the children are grown—and then sell the house and split the proceeds.

Susan and Martin bought their house 30 years ago for $15,000. Over the years, they have made $20,000 of improvements. Their tax basis is now $35,000.

If they sell it for $420,000, their taxable gain would be $385,000. If they sell it together, they can exclude the entire gain.

If Susan becomes sole owner of the house before it is sold, after the $250,000 exclusion, her taxable gain is $135,000. Thus, without proper planning, she could end up owing $27,000 in federal taxes.

Whether you should choose joint ownership depends on the personal and financial factors involved. For example, if you have custody of the children, it may be best for you to keep the house at least a few more years to keep changes to a minimum for the children.

If you decide on this arrangement, you must get a written agreement or court order granting you exclusive use of the residence and keep his name on the deed. The house will then be considered his primary residence, and he will preserve his ability to exclude $250,000 of gain when the house is sold.

Although joint ownership can make settling easier, you will need to consider if you really want to continue to maintain financial ties with your spouse. After the divorce, your goals and needs will change. It is usually best to cut as many ties as you can. The less financial involvement you and your ex have, the less chance there is for disagreement and misunderstanding and the easier it will be to get on with your life.

## Determining the Value of Your Home

Whatever method you use, you will need to determine the value of your home. The value of the house is determined by its fair market value. In many states, sales commissions and other costs of sale won't be deducted from that value, since the house isn't being sold and those costs won't be incurred.

You can determine the value of a house in a number of ways.

- Have the house appraised by a professional appraiser. Even if you recently refinanced your home, don't rely on the value from the mortgage company's appraisal. Such appraisals are often low, to protect the bank and limit its losses in the event it has to foreclose.

- Ask a real estate agent to provide you with the price of homes that recently sold in your neighborhood and the listing prices of homes currently on the market to generate your own informed estimate.

- Agree on a value that is acceptable to both you and your spouse. Any reasonable method that you choose should be acceptable to the court.

## Small Businesses

A business started during the marriage with joint funds is considered marital property. Businesses started with separate funds, or already in operation at the time of marriage, create a more complex situation. Although the rules vary, in most states a portion of the business will be considered a marital asset. The marital portion may be the amount of joint funds used to expand an existing business plus the appreciation attributed to that contribution. In addition, the efforts of the spouse who operated the business may have contributed to the growth of the business during the marriage, and thus may have created marital value.

A business appraiser will likely start with the balance sheet for the business, which lists all of the assets and liabilities. Then the appraiser will adjust the value of the assets to their current market value, not their cost. For example, the value of equipment will likely be adjusted down to account for wear and tear, and real estate will likely be adjusted up for appreciation.

The appraiser will also add assets and liabilities not on the balance sheet. For example, the value of customer lists, patents, work in progress, future contracts, and below-market leases may need to be added as assets. Pending lawsuits may need to be shown as liabilities.

If you have not been intimately involved in the business and do not have complete access to business records, you will probably have a hard time obtaining accurate information for these asset categories unless you subpoena documents during the discovery process.

Valuing a business is a very complex task, and a professional appraiser is often required, particularly when the business has a lot of goodwill value. In some states, a business has goodwill if it has net profits that exceed a fair wage to the owner of the business. In others, a business has goodwill if it can be sold for more than the value of its assets. Your attorney or a business valuation expert can help you determine the value of the business and advise you on the law in your state.

## CHAPTER 7

# Retirement Plans and Social Security

Believe it or not, all retirement plans and pension benefits acquired during the marriage are marital property, even only one name is on the account and the benefits won't be paid for many years. Even if you have never worked, you probably have a right to retirement benefits in your ex's name. This chapter will help you figure out what types of plans you have, and how best to divide them.

## Plan Valuation

Retirement plans come in many different shapes and sizes. Here is how you can find out how much your retirement plans are worth:

### Individual Retirement Accounts (IRAs)

IRAs are easy to value—simply add the amounts you've contributed plus all earnings of the account. But you really don't need to do that yourself—at least once a year, the IRA custodian sends a statement showing the value of the account on that date.

## Defined Contribution Plans

Employee savings plans, 401(k) plans, 403(b) plans, and tax-sheltered annuities (TSAs) are valued just like IRAs. Most plan administrators issue quarterly statements.

## Defined Benefit Plans

A defined benefit plan provides a monthly retirement benefit based on your highest annual earnings and the length of time you were employed by the company. Defined benefit plans are different from other types of plans because there is not a pot of cash sitting there from which you can withdraw your entire portion today. A defined benefit plan is merely the promise of a future stream of income calculated using a formula that takes into account the employee's years of service and earnings.

---

Fred and Martha are getting a divorce.

He has informed her that he will receive $2,200 per month when he retires. She decides that a couple of thousand dollars twenty years from now is not worth fighting over—she would rather get the $9,500 grand piano.

Did Martha make a good decision?

Well, no. The present value of $2,200 a month for the rest of Fred's life is nearly $250,000!

Instead of taking the piano, Martha can trade out her half up front and take $125,000 of another asset, leaving Fred with his pension; or she can wait until Fred retires and get one-half of the marital portion of the benefit.

Martha needs good advice from her attorney, accountant, or financial professional to understand the pros and cons of any decision she makes.

---

The company may provide you with a calculation of the cash value of the retirement plan. But often the true value of the retirement payments you will receive is considerably higher than the cash value of the plan. Have the pension valued by an actuary or divorce financial professional to determine its true worth.

## Vesting

Vested amounts are those that are available to the employee if he or she leaves the company. Amounts that you or your spouse contributed to retirement plans, plus the earnings on those amounts, are always 100 percent vested. Employer contributions to the plan may or may not be fully vested. This means that you currently own only part of the funds set aside for your benefit, and must continue working for the company to become entitled to all of the money in the plan.

---

Fred works for a company where he is 30 percent vested in a 401(k) plan.

Fred's 401(k) is worth $18,600 today.

Of that amount, Fred contributed $12,500, which has earned $1,300 in interest over the years.

His employer has contributed $4,000 to Fred's 401(k) and that portion has earned $800 in interest over the years.

If Fred is 30 percent vested and decides to leave the company, he can take 100 percent of his own contributions and earnings ($12,500 + $1,300 = $13,800) and 30 percent of the total value of the employer contribution and earnings ($4,000 + $800 = $4,800), which is $1,440 ($4,800 x 30% = $1,440), for a total of $13,800 + $1,440 = $15,240.

---

# Retirement Plan Division

When dividing retirement plans, you have three options: each of you keeps the plans in your own names, divide the plans now, or (for pension plans) divide them at retirement. Let's consider each of these options:

## Keep Plans in Your Own Names

The simplest option is for each of you to keep the plans in your own name and divide other property to make up the difference. If this option appeals to you, be sure to take taxes into account. Money in retirement accounts generally is worth less than money in the bank or home equity, since the retirement funds will be taxable when withdrawn. Reduce the value of such accounts by the taxes you eventually will pay to see if you are receiving a fair share.

## Dividing IRAs

IRAs can be divided by sending a copy of your divorce agreement to the IRA custodian. Be sure to have the IRA funds paid directly from the IRA custodian to your IRA. If you receive distributions from an IRA and do not roll them over within 60 days, you will owe income taxes on the distribution, plus a 10 percent penalty if you are under age 59-1/2. If you are dividing an IRA, you should have your share of the investments transferred to an account at the same brokerage firm to reduce administrative headaches. Later the funds can be transferred wherever you want.

## Dividing Other Plans

Other retirement plans are a bit more complicated. Splitting retirement plans that are covered by ERISA, such as 401(k)s and pension plans, requires a legal document called a Qualified Domestic Relations Order (QDRO, pronounced "kwa-dro"). A QDRO is a court order that must be served on (delivered to) the administrator for the plan. Drafting a QDRO requires special knowledge and should be done by a QDRO specialist.

The QDRO may provide that part of the retirement funds that your husband has in defined contribution plans, such as 401(k)s, be distributed to an IRA in your name. For defined benefit plans, the QDRO will provide that you will receive payments once your ex reaches retirement age. Then the plan administrator will begin make monthly payments to you based on your life expectancy or other options you will choose at that time.

## Transferring Plan Assets to Your IRA

If the plan allows, the plan administrator can be directed to distribute your portion to an existing IRA or one newly created for this purpose. If you choose this option, be sure to request that the distribution be made directly to your IRA. If you receive a distribution directly from a retirement plan, the plan administrator will withhold 20 percent of the proceeds for federal income taxes. You can avoid this through a direct rollover into your IRA.

## Paying Plan Assets Directly to You

All or a part of the funds in your ex's retirement account can be paid directly to you, if the retirement plan allows it. You can either keep the money and pay tax on it now, or roll it into an IRA within 60 days. The plan administrator will withhold 20 percent for federal income tax from the distribution, and you may owe more taxes when you file your income tax return. You won't owe a 10 percent early-distribution penalty even if you are under 59-1/2, since the distribution is made using a QDRO.

If you are in a low tax bracket in the year you receive a QDRO distribution, consider keeping a portion of the QDRO distribution and paying tax on that portion at your low rate, rather than rolling the full amount of the QDRO distribution into your IRA. To decide whether or not to do this, you will need to estimate your taxable income for the year of the distribution. If you are in a low tax bracket, you can save taxes by keeping the portion of the distribution that would be taxed at that low bracket, and rolling the rest into an IRA. An accountant or financial professional can help you determine the best option for you.

Jake and Jennifer are getting a divorce.

Jake, age 50, is software engineer whose 401(k) is worth $280,000.

Jennifer, age 51, will get half, or $140,000, of the 401(k) in the divorce settlement.

Jennifer needs $80,000 right now to pay her attorney, fix the roof, and pay credit card debt.

She instructs the plan administrator to send her $80,000 in cash and transfer the remainder to her IRA.

Because the plan will withhold 20 percent to pay her taxes on this amount, she will need to ask for $100,000. They will withhold $20,000 (20 percent) and send her the remaining $80,000. There will be $40,000 left to send to her IRA.

She will not have to pay the 10 percent penalty on withdrawing the cash even though she is under age 59-1/2 because the division is pursuant to a QDRO.

## Survivor Benefits

Survivor benefits are very important, in case your spouse dies before you can get the QDRO drawn up. Survivor benefits that will pay you in the event of his death can be set up before retirement–even for an ex-spouse.

If you choose to receive the benefits after retirement, you will need to determine what will happen if your spouse dies before he is eligible to retire. Each pension plan has different rules on the subject, and needs to be evaluated by a pension plan expert. In some cases, the pension will pay out money to you as the surviving ex-spouse, and in others, the pension simply disappears, leaving you with nothing.

To make sure that your settlement takes effect even if your spouse dies before retirement, get your QDRO done as soon as possible. Talk to your attorney about having the QDRO drawn up to have ready for the court to approve at the same time as your final decree.

## Military Retirement

Military personnel are eligible to receive retirement pay if they have served for 20 years or longer. The treatment of military retired pay differs from state to state. In most community property states (Arizona, California, Idaho, Louisiana, Nevada, New Mexico, Texas, Washington and Wisconsin), a portion of the military spouse's retired pay is considered the property of both spouses. The non-military spouse will be entitled to one-half of the retiree's benefits during the marriage, calculated as the number of years of marriage during which the retired pay was earned, divided by the total years of service.

---

Joan was married to Bob for 10 years of his 20-year military career. Joan and Bob are getting a divorce.

If he is entitled to $2,000 per month in disposable military retirement pay, she is entitled to one-half of the benefits multiplied by 10/20 (10 years of marriage/20 years of service).

Therefore, she is entitled to receive $500 per month.

---

If the spouses were married for at least ten years while the member was on active duty, the non-military spouse will qualify for direct enforcement, which means that her portion of the retired pay will be paid directly to her by the military finance office.

Most non-community property states will award a portion of the retired pay to the non-military spouse. A few states treat military retired pay as the property only of the military person. However, the judge must consider the retired pay received by the military spouse when setting the amount of alimony in those states.

A quirk in a US Supreme Court decision saves the military spouse money at the expense of the non-military spouse. The court ruled that family courts can divide only *disposable* retired pay. That means that the amount of the monthly military pension is first reduced by income tax and any other necessary withholdings. The net amount is then divided. Even if the non-military spouse were awarded 50 percent of the pension by the courts, she would *actually receive less than 50 percent* because the monthly payment would be based on the net, rather than the gross, retirement plan.

---

Jack and Carol have been married for the entire 20 years of his military career.

Jack's gross pay is $2,000 with $500 withheld for income taxes, leaving $1,500 net pay.

At retirement, Carol will receive one-half of the $1,500, or $750, and Jack will receive $750.

Although this seems like an equal division, the inequities become obvious at tax time. Carol computed her income taxes on the $750 received, but gets no credit for withholding. This means she will owe income taxes, reducing her payment even more.

Jack will pay tax on $1,250 ($2,000 gross pay, less $750 diverted to Carol), but will be able to claim the $500 of income tax withheld on his tax return—so he will probably be entitled to a tax refund based on his military retirement pay.

---

## Military Survivor Benefit Plan (SPB)

Military Survivor Benefit Plan survivor benefits, known as SBP, are available to the spouse or former spouse of any retiring member. Enrollment in the SBP plan is automatic unless the member and his spouse agree in writing to reduce or waive coverage.

When a retired military member divorces, he is required to notify the appropriate Finance Center that handles pay for his branch of the military. The military will terminate the coverage under SBP, and he will receive a refund for all payments that he made for coverage since the divorce. A special rule allows the retiree to reinstate his former spouse (and minor children) as beneficiaries, if both spouses sign a reinstatement application and submit it to the appropriate Finance Center within one year of the date of divorce. Similarly, an active duty member may agree to name his ex-spouse as beneficiary of the SBP when he retires.

## Medical, Commissary and Exchange privileges

Full medical, commissary and exchange privileges are available for an ex-spouse if the military member served 20 years, and the spouses were married for 20 years while the member was on active duty. If the military member served 20 years and the spouses were married for 20 years, but the member was on active duty only 15 to 19 of those years during the marriage, the ex-spouse will be entitled only to medical care for a limited period of time.

After that limited time, she will have 90 days to enroll in a group health plan established by the Department of Defense. A divorced spouse is not entitled to medical, commissary or exchange privileges if the marriage was less than 20 years or the military spouse served less than 20 years.

# Other Retirement Plans

## Public Employees Retirement System (PERS)

These plans are used by many state and local governments, and in some areas, for employees of public educational institutions. Some plans permit the ex-spouse to receive benefits at retirement, while others do not.

Others will allow the creation of a separate account in each spouse's name. If neither of these options is available, it is best divide other assets to make up the difference or to get a court order to compel your ex to send you a share of his benefits as they are received.

## Federal Employee Retirement System (FERS) and Civil Service Retirement System (CSRS)

FERS is administered by the Office of Personnel Management, under its own set of rules. In general, you can receive your share of your spouse's retirement after he retires. You cannot elect early retirement and cannot receive an annuity based on your own life expectancy.

## Section 457 Plans

A Section 457 plan is used for some state and local government workers. These plans cannot pay benefits to you before your ex leaves the job, reaches age 70-1/2, or has an unforeseeable emergency (which does not include divorce!)

A lump-sum payment from a Section 457 plan cannot be rolled over tax-free to an IRA, as could a similar distribution from a 401(k). In addition, in non-community property states, your ex would be taxed on all distributions that you receive. In community property states, half of the distributions would likely be taxable to each of you.

## Stock Options

A stock option gives the holder the right to purchase shares of the employer's stock now or later, at a price already set. If the stock rises in value, the holder can still buy it at the set price, which could be considerably below the trading price.

The stock option has a value. It is the difference between the current price of the stock and the set price at which it can be purchased. The option has no current value if the option price is higher than the current price of the stock. However, it would have value in the future if the price of the stock goes up.

You have two choices for including the option in your division of assets. One choice is to value the option, leave it with the spouse to whom the option is granted, and give the other spouse an asset of similar value. A second choice—which may be fairer if the non-employee spouse thinks the stock will substantially rise in value in the future—is for the spouses to continue to hold the option together, and then exercise the option jointly to buy the stock in the future. Some employers will allow options to be transferred into the name of the non-employee spouse.

Some state laws specify that if the rights to the options have not yet vested (that is, the employee spouse does not yet have the right to exercise the option to buy), then the stock option is not marital property and is not subject to division by the courts at divorce. Consult with your attorney if stock options are significant to your marital estate.

## Social Security

If you were married for ten years or longer, you will be eligible to collect Social Security benefits based on your ex-spouse's earnings record when you reach retirement age, assuming you are not married to someone else at the time. Those benefits are equal to one-half the amount your former spouse is eligible to collect. The benefits are based on your spouse's earnings over his entire career, including the years after your marriage was dissolved. If you are divorcing a person with great future earnings potential and you've been married nearly ten years, consider sticking it out a little longer or delay finalizing the divorce until after the ten-year mark.

You can collect benefits as long as they don't exceed the benefits you receive on your own earnings. Even if he remarries, you will still be entitled to a benefit equal to half of his Social Security.

To help explain these complicated rules, let's follow the story of Ted, Susie, Cathy and Frank.

Ted and Susie were married for 14 years. They are now getting divorced.

Ted is entitled at age 65 to receive $750 per month in Social Security, based on his earnings.

Susie is entitled at age 65 to receive $250 per month in Social Security, based on her earnings.

Based on Ted's earnings, Susie will be eligible to receive $375 a month, half of his benefit. Whether or not she chooses this benefit has no effect on his monthly check.

Since $375 is greater than $250, Susie will likely choose to receive benefits based on Ted's earnings. If Susie's earned benefits were $450 per month, she would likely choose to receive benefits based on her own earnings. Sorry—she can't have both.

If Ted later marries Cathy and they are married for 11 years before getting a divorce, Cathy would also be entitled to receive $375 per month based on Ted's earnings.

No matter how many women he marries, Ted still gets his $750 per month.

If Susie remarries, to a man we'll call Frank, she will be entitled to collect spousal benefits based on his earnings history if they stay married. She will not be entitled to benefits based on Ted's earnings.

If she divorces Frank after being married to him for 10 years or longer, she will be able to receive benefits based on the earning histories of *either* Ted *or* Frank *or* her own account, whichever is higher.

If Ted dies before Susie marries Frank, she will be entitled to widow's benefits, which approximate his full Social Security benefit if she waits to collect until her full retirement age of 65-67, and 71.5% if she receives benefits at age 60. As long as she does not remarry before age 60, she will get a widow's benefit. (And Cathy will also receive widow's benefits!)

And you thought the folks at the Social Security office looked like they had nothing to do!

# CHAPTER 8

# Debts and Unusual Assets

---

Now that we've got the big stuff out of the way, let's focus on dividing the rest of your marital estate, including your debt and some often-overlooked assets, such as vacation pay and frequent flyer miles. In this chapter, we discuss how you can best divide your debt and protect yourself from your partner's debts. We'll also discuss how to divide unusual assets.

## Debts

### Debts After You Separate

A separation won't free you from paying any of the debts that are in your name, even if the money was spent by your spouse without your knowledge or consent. This is because a separation agreement is a contract between you and your spouse . The bank or finance company has a separate contract with each person who signed for the debt, and will try to collect from both of you in case of default. If your spouse promises to pay some of the bills and then doesn't, your only recourse is to sue your ex for breach of contract—but you will still have to make the payments on the debt, and your credit rating will still be affected.

## Consider Your Options

As you and your spouse negotiate your settlement, you can choose among these options for dealing with the debts you incurred together:

• You can use joint funds, or sell property you jointly own, to pay off your debts.

• You can divide your property and your debts equally and each of you will be responsible for repaying the debts assigned to you.

• One of you can agree to pay the bulk of the debts and, in exchange, receive a greater share of the marital property or increased alimony as an offset.

The first option is the safest, as it will extinguish the debt. The second and third options are risky—your ex-spouse may not pay the debts assigned to him. If you choose the second or third option, your agreement is between you and your ex-spouse only. Creditors can still look to you for repayment of marital debts even though your spouse agrees to pay the bills in your settlement agreement.

---

Jason and Amanda fought over financial issues all the time, mostly over Jason's lack of control of his spending habits.

After he replaced their big screen TV with a slightly bigger screen TV for the fifth time, they finally decided to divorce.

Jason and Amanda agreed that he would take the $9,000 credit card debt he had incurred on their joint VISA card.

After the divorce, Jason decided he needed a new couch to go with the TV, and didn't pay off the credit card.

Because Amanda's name was also on the card, VISA sued Amanda for payment.

---

## Restructure Remaining Debt

If you can't pay off debts with joint funds, one or both of you are going to have to assume the debt and repay it in the future. If you and your spouse have good credit, you should each apply for credit cards in your own names. You can then each transfer the balances of the debt you assume to your own credit cards, and cancel all joint credit cards.

## Get Help If You Need It

If debts are a problem for you during or after divorce, consider calling Consumer Credit Counseling Service for help. CCCS is a national nonprofit organization with offices in every state. For a nominal fee (which is often waived), CCCS can help you create a budget. If you have enough monthly income, CCCS will set up a repayment plan for you under which you make one payment to CCCS each month and CCCS sends money to each of your creditors.

Each CCCS office is funded by major creditors, such as banks and department stores, by retaining a small percentage of the money you pay them. CCCS can waive late fees, over-limit fees, and some interest charges on your debt. CCCS may not recommend bankruptcy— even if it's appropriate for you—because in bankruptcy, the creditors who fund them may not get paid.

Nevertheless, most people find CCCS very helpful. You can find the office nearest you by calling 800-388-2227. Under no circumstances should you use a for-profit credit repair organization or company that demands a large up-front payment. They cannot do anything for you that CCCS cannot do, for a much lower fee.

## Consider Bankruptcy

Money problems often contribute to marriage problems, and vice versa, so it is not unusual for people contemplating divorce to be contemplating bankruptcy at the same time.

If bankruptcy seems to be the best answer for your debt burden, and you haven't yet divorced, you must decide whether to divorce or go

bankrupt first. In general, if both spouses are considering bankruptcy—
and they probably should be if they are both liable for all the debts—
filing for bankruptcy separately after divorce will cost more in filing
fees and attorney fees. It may also be more fair to both spouses if the
bankruptcy comes before the assets and debts are split in divorce, especially considering what happened to Sarah and Jeff.

---

Sarah and Jeff were married for fifteen years.

Their primary asset is their home, and they also have a great deal
of debt. If Jeff agrees to assume most of the debts in exchange
for keeping the house, Sarah will end up with very little in the
property settlement.

If he then declares bankruptcy after the divorce, the debt
will be discharged, and he will be allowed to keep most or
all of the equity in the home. Sarah has nothing and Jeff has the
house.

Things could be worse. Here's how. This time, Jeff takes the
house and the debts, but gives Sarah a note for her share of the
equity, secured by the house. When Jeff declares bankruptcy after
the divorce, the debts—including quite possibly the note due
Sarah—will be discharged, and Jeff will probably be allowed to
keep most or all of the equity in the home. If Sarah decides to
take a note from Jeff, she should have it drafted by an attorney
familiar with bankruptcy law who can prevent it from being
discharged if Jeff decides to go "BK."

---

Here's one good piece of news—if your ex-spouse files for bankruptcy
after your divorce, you may be able to keep your alimony or child support. He cannot discharge any alimony or child support owed to you
under a separation agreement, divorce decree or court order or property settlement, except in the following two situations:

- Support owed under a state's general support law, not a court order. If your ex-spouse is paying you under the general law of your state that requires parents to support their children, or spouses to support each other, and no court actually ordered the support, the debt is dischargeable.

- Support owed someone other than a spouse, ex-spouse, child, or child welfare agency. If you have assigned the right to receive the support to someone else, or a creditor has garnished the payments, the debt is dischargeable.

A court order setting the amount of child support payments is clear enough to prevent discharge in bankruptcy. Some other debts, however, may also be considered non-dischargeable child support or alimony. The most common are marital debts—the debts a spouse was ordered to pay when the couple divorced.

Obligations that are generally considered support (and aren't dischargeable) include debts that:

- Are paid to a spouse who is maintaining the primary residence of the children while there is a serious imbalance of incomes

- Terminate on the death or remarriage of the recipient spouse

- Depend on the future income of either spouse

- Are paid in installments over a substantial period of time.

## Other Assets

Consider these often-overlooked assets that can be divided in divorce, and be sure to get your share. You may find that you have more divide than you knew!

### Life Insurance

Review any whole life or universal life insurance policies to determine their cash value. If the policy was purchased or premiums were paid with marital property, the cash value is marital property. If all premiums were paid with one spouse's separate funds or by a business belonging to only one spouse, the policy is generally considered separate property.

Do not confuse the death benefit with cash value. Cash value is found in "permanent" policies such as whole life or universal life. Term life insurance does not have cash value. However, some attorneys will argue that a large insurance policy on someone who can no longer buy insurance should be considered in final negotiations.

## Safe Deposit Boxes

Be careful about removing the contents of the box yourself. Your spouse may allege that you have appropriated property that belonged to both of you, and will probably create unnecessary hard feelings between you.

To secure the box during the divorce, you way want to ask your spouse for the other key, or give both keys to the bank for safekeeping.

If neither of these solutions is feasible, you can file papers for a restraining order to prevent your spouse from having access to the box. If you choose this option, be sure to serve a copy of the restraining order to the bank or other safe deposit box custodian.

In some states, restraining orders are automatically put in place when you file for divorce. If that is the case in your state, and you have filed for divorce, you need only serve the safe deposit box custodian with notice of the restraining order to prevent access to the box. Automatic restraining orders are generally reciprocal, however, so be aware that you will be restrained from access to the safe deposit box as well.

## Bonuses and Other Payments

Be aware of any bonuses your spouse receives in the first year after separation. Bonuses paid soon after separation were probably earned during the marriage. In that case, the bonus might be considered marital or community property and you would therefore be entitled to a share of it.

## Hobbies or Side Businesses

Be sure to value hobbies or side businesses that may generate income. The tools, supplies, and goodwill of hobby businesses have value that should be considered during the divorce.

Samantha's soon-to-be-ex refurbishes antique cars and sells them at car shows, local auto dealers, and Internet auction sites. The assets of this business include equipment and supplies used to refurbish the cars, as well as the cars themselves.

The equipment and inventories are marital assets, and the business may be lucrative enough to have some goodwill value as well.

In most cases, Samantha is entitled to a share of these assets in divorce.

## Career Assets

If you have a PHT degree (Putting Honey Through), be sure to total up the costs you paid for your spouse to obtain an education. Depending on the laws of your state, you may have a right to be compensated for the cost of the education, the degree may be considered marital property, or you may be entitled to support based on the money you paid.

Career assets include education, licenses, degrees, job experience, seniority, life insurance, health insurance, disability insurance, unemployment benefits, Social Security, paid sick leave, vacation pay, a network of professional contacts, and so forth. Although career assets have value, it can't always be quantified. Too often, career assets are not taken into account in divorce settlements.

Some states regard degrees or professional designations as marital assets, and some do not. In any case, the increased earning power derived from education is given weight in final property division decisions.

## Frequent Flyer Miles

Believe it or not, frequent flyer miles are considered marital assets, and can be divided in divorce. If you want to divide your frequent flyer miles, consider these options:

- Some frequent flyer programs allow spouses to transfer points between their accounts.

- Some programs allow free tickets to be issued in the name of someone other than the frequent flyer.

- You can value the miles at 1-1/2 or 2 cents per mile and divide other assets to make up the difference.

## Vacation Pay

Although you can't take your spouse's vacation for him, in some states, the accumulated vacation days can be valued based on your spouse's earnings. You can then take a corresponding amount of other marital property.

## Season Tickets

If you have season tickets to the ballpark, theatre, or symphony, you probably do not want to split them with your ex, because you would end up sitting side by side at the event. Generally, the spouse who has the most interest in the activity will bargain with the other spouse to acquire his or her rights to the tickets in exchange for other assets.

If both of you want the tickets, you could draw straws, or perhaps use joint money to purchase another set of tickets of equal value, so that each of you can have a pair of tickets. You could agree to alternate use the tickets, but that is generally not satisfying to an avid fan who has spent years building priority on particular events.

## Club Memberships

If you and your spouse belong to an athletic or country club for which you paid an initiation fee, and only one of you wants to continue the membership, you can value your membership at the price it currently costs to join. The spouse wanting the membership takes it and the other spouse takes other property of similar value. If both of you want to continue membership, many clubs will split memberships of divorcing spouses, for a fee.

## Timeshares

Unfortunately, the current value of the timeshare may be less than was paid for it, and perhaps even less than you and your spouse still owe on it. In fact, neither of you may want it. If that is the case, you have several options:

- One of you can take it at no cost.

- You can continue to own it jointly.

- You can try to sell it.

- You can deed it back to the financing institution.

Not all timeshares are financial disasters and one or both of you may want it. If only one of you wants it, then simply give the other spouse a similarly valued item in exchange. If you both want it, you can continue to own it jointly and each use it half the allotted time every year or alternate use of the property each year.

## Household Goods

Value household goods at garage sale prices. A good rule of thumb is 20 percent of the retail price of the item. You can make a list of all of your assets and divide them according to who wants or needs them, while trying to balance your division to 50-50.

## Prepaid Expenses

Prepaid magazine subscriptions, professional dues, and the like are marital property. If you prepaid for several years, these items could have measurable value to add to the marital property to be divided.

Generally, insurance –be it life, disability or casualty—is prepaid in quarterly, semi-annual or annual premiums. You and your spouse may be covered personally under life and disability policies and your real estate and automobiles may be covered under casualty policies for which substantial premiums have been prepaid. Consider these pre-payments when dividing your property.

---

Beth prepaid $1,000 for one year's coverage of car insurance for their jointly-owned car three months ago.

There are still nine months of insurance that have already been paid. This means that $750 of the premium is still prepaid. The spouse who gives up the car should be reimbursed $375, or half of the prepaid premiums.

---

## Disability Insurance

In some cases, disability insurance proceeds can be considered a marital asset. For example, if both spouses paid the premiums on the disability insurance during the marriage, one spouse became disabled during the marriage, and the disability benefits were intended to be used as retirement funds, benefits were considered to be marital property. Consult an attorney if this is significant in your situation.

## Employee "Perks"

Perquisites of employment, such as employee discounts, working condition fringe benefits, de minimis fringe benefits, and meals and lodging (in certain cases), are nontaxable. However, if their value is significant, they may be considered in the divorce settlement.

## Medical Savings Accounts

Medical Savings Accounts are treated just like IRAs in divorce. That is, they can be divided by a Marital Settlement Agreement at the time of divorce, and the division is non-taxable to both spouses.

# CHAPTER 9

# Tax Issues

The tax man cometh—and he doesn't stop cometh-ing after divorce. In this section, we address the many tax issues you face—filing status, tax refunds, how to file tax returns, what you can deduct, and how to protect yourself from past tax liabilities.

## Filing Status

If you are still married on the last day of the year—that is, your divorce won't become final until the next calendar year—you have three options for filing your tax returns. You can file jointly, married filing separately or head of household (if you qualify). If you are divorced by the last day of the year, you can either file as single, or as head of household, if you qualify.

- Head of household—You can file as head of household even though you are not divorced or legally separated if you live apart and meet certain tests. You can also file as head of household after your divorce is final.

- Married filing jointly—You can file jointly if you are still married, even though you are living apart, if you do not have a court order of divorce or separate maintenance. If you both agree to file jointly, you'll report your combined income and deduct your combined allowable expenses. If you decide to file jointly or have already filed a joint return, be sure you have a written agreement designating how you will share any refunds or taxes due on the joint tax return. Include this agreement in your settlement agreement.

- Married filing separately—If you are still married but do not have a court order of divorce or separate maintenance, you may file a separate return reporting only your income and deducting only your expenses. You often pay more in taxes by filing this way, but it may be worth it if you question your spouse's integrity in filing tax returns. If you file separately, you can always amend returns within three years to file jointly. The reverse is not true, however—once you file a joint return, you cannot amend it to file separately.

---

Janis and Andy were divorced on December 31. Since they were married for all but the last day of the year, they decided to file their income tax return jointly.

Since the IRS only recognizes their status on the last day of the year, the IRS considers them divorced for the year and won't allow them to file jointly.

---

## Use Head of Household

If you qualify and file as head of household instead of single or as married filing separately, your standard deduction will be higher. In addition, your tax rates will be lower than the rates for single or married filing separately and you may be able to claim the earned income credit.

You can choose head of household filing status if you meet all of the following conditions. (NOTE: It is possible for each spouse to file as head of household if there are at least two children and both spouses meet all of the qualifications.)

- You paid more than half of the cost of maintaining your home for the tax year

- Your spouse did not live in your home during the last six months of the tax year

- Your home was the primary home of your child for more than six months of the year

- You are allowed to claim that child as a dependent (although you can waive that right and let the other parent claim the exemption)

## Marriage Tax Penalty

An attorney or financial advisor may recommend that you delay finalizing your divorce until January so you can file a joint tax return for the year prior to the divorce. However, filing a joint return may cost more in taxes, not less, especially if you and your spouse have similar incomes. That's because of the marriage tax penalty, an inequity in the tax rate schedules that causes married people to pay more in taxes than single people if both have similar levels of income.

## When to File Separately

### When You Doubt Your Ex's Honesty

If you file separate returns while you are married, you are responsible only for the tax due on your own return. By filing separately, you ensure that you will not be held liable for the actions of your spouse, if he omits income or overstates expenses. However, in many cases the total tax liability for the couple will be higher if you file separately.

If you are separated but not yet divorced, and you doubt your spouse's honesty in reporting income or deductions to the IRS, don't file a joint return. Both spouses are responsible for all income on a joint return. If your spouse omits income, the IRS could—and probably would—come after you for payment.

Protect yourself from paying taxes on income you know nothing about. Although you might owe more for the tax year in question if you file separately than if you file jointly, in the long run your filing separately could save you a bundle.

## When It Will Save You Money

You and your spouse can file joint income tax returns if you are still married at midnight on December 31. For couples still married on December 31, it is simpler to file a joint return than to file two separate tax returns. However, there may be an advantage to separate returns. The income for the year will be allocated to the person who earned it. Filing a joint return means the spouse who had little income may pay more taxes on a joint return than she would pay if the spouses filed separate returns.

Of course, if you file a separate return and you are receiving taxable alimony (see Chapter 4 on Alimony and Separate Maintenance for the rules for taxable alimony) you will have to report that income on your separate return. If you are paying tax-deductible alimony, you will be able to deduct it on your return.

## File an Extension

It may make sense to file an extension to allow time for a full evaluation of the best way to file. You will need to pay any taxes due when you file the extension. When you file your tax return, you will claim credit for this tax payment and you can seek a refund of any overpayment.

The automatic extension lasts until August 15. If you are still not ready to file, compete IRS Form 2688, Application for Additional Extension of Time to File U.S. Individual Income Tax. You must file this by August 15 and state your "'good cause" for needing more time for filing your return. If your extension is granted, you have until October 15 to file your return.

Harry moved out on New Year's Day and sent Sally and their son support all year long.

Since there was no court order or written agreement, the support he paid was not deductible by him nor taxable to Sally.

Sally earned $20,000 for the year and had $6,000 federal income tax withheld. Harry's salary was $80,000, including his bonus, and his withholding was $17,000.

Harry offers Sally a deal. If they file jointly, they will owe $20,256 in federal taxes. Their combined withholding was $23,000, so they will receive a refund of $2,744. He will split it according to their income, and send Sally a check for one-fifth ($549).

Is this a good deal for Sally?

Sally is entitled to file as head of household because she supported her son for more than half of the year. On her $20,000 total income, she owes only $1,571 in federal taxes and would receive a refund of $4,429.

Harry, however, wouldn't be in such good shape. As a married person filing separately, he owes a total of $19,761 in taxes. With only $17,000 withheld, he must pay the IRS an additional $2,761.

If Sally wants to be fair, she can offer to split the refunds and obligations equally (despite their unequal incomes), they would be much better off filing jointly. Then, they'd each be entitled to $1,372 ($2,744 halved). This is a better deal overall. Filing separately, the net refund (Sally's refund less Harry's obligation) is only $1,668. Filing jointly (remember), it was $2,744. Filing jointly results in a savings of over $1,000, which Harry and Sally can divide.

# Deduct Legal Fees

Most legal fees and court costs for getting a divorce are considered personal and are not deductible on your income tax return. The Internal Revenue Code lets you deduct, as a miscellaneous expense, any money paid for advice concerning the tax consequences of your divorce or for securing alimony. (The reverse is not true: legal costs for attempting to reduce support payments or to defend against a claim for greater support are not deductible.) Fees may be paid to any attorney, accountant, mediator, financial professional, or other consultant.

A portion of the legal expenses that are not currently tax deductible may be added to the tax basis and become deductible when you sell assets you receive. Legal fees that you pay to negotiate the property settlement can be allocated among the assets you receive in proportion to their value. When you later sell those assets, you can then deduct the legal expenses from the sales price. You must be able to show that those fees were for time spent defending title to assets or obtaining them for you. For example, the cost of preparing and filing a deed to put title to a property in your name alone can be added to the tax basis of the property, and reduces your gain when the property is sold.

In order for you to claim a deduction for legal expenses incurred in a divorce, the attorney must make a reasonable allocation of the legal expenses between deductible and non-deductible advice. Ask your attorney to divide your bill into three parts:

- Fees relating to tax advice and alimony that are currently deductible

- Fees relating to property settlement

- Fees that are non-deductible.

## Paying Your Legal Fees

While it is tempting to pay legal fees from your business, don't. Most divorce costs are not tax deductible, and paying the expenses from your business may make it possible for your spouse's attorney to join the business in the lawsuit and scrutinize its records in detail.

Rather than having your ex pay your legal fees, which would not be deductible, he might be better off paying additional alimony to you to cover the legal fees. He can even make the additional alimony payment directly to your attorney, as long as the divorce agreement calls for payment to a third party.

## Fees Paid to Other Professionals

Any fees paid to specialized professionals, such as tax attorneys, accountants or financial professionals for tax and investment advice are fully deductible even if they aren't specifically related to your property settlement. If you pay an accountant to help you determine the tax ramifications of your divorce decisions, the entire accountant's bill is deductible. Likewise, fees paid to a financial planner for advice concerning investments and financial goals are deductible.

# Other Tax Issues

## Handling Past Tax Liabilities

If you file a joint return you may be held liable for all prior taxes, even if your spouse earned all the income and prepared the tax return. Generally, both people who sign a joint return are jointly and individually liable for any tax, interest, or penalty that may be due. You are also liable after your divorce for returns filed before the divorce.

If you believe your spouse may have omitted income or overstated deductions on prior joint tax returns filed by the two of you, make sure your settlement agreement includes an indemnification clause. In an indemnification clause, your spouse agrees to be responsible for any back taxes, and further agrees to repay you if the IRS collects those back taxes from you.

If you can convince the IRS that you were an innocent spouse who knew nothing about the tax understatement, the IRS may determine that you are not liable for the taxes due. Convincing the IRS that you are an innocent spouse is not an easy task. If you find yourself in this situation, consult a tax advisor immediately.

## Taxes and Children

The exemption for your children generally goes to the custodial parent. If you share joint custody, the exemption goes to the parent who has the child the greatest number of days. You can specify another arrangement in your divorce agreement if you like.

Include personal exemptions, filing status, and other tax consequences of your children in your divorce agreement. Detailing them in your agreement at the beginning will avoid costly trips to court to settle the issues later. When negotiating these tax issues with your ex, remember that the child tax credit and the education tax credits are only available to the parent who claims the exemptions.

If you will be the non-custodial parent and you will claim the tax exemption for the children, ask your spouse to sign IRS Form 8332 (Release of Claim to Exemption for Child of Divorced or Separated Parents) when your divorce papers are finalized. You will file this form every year with your tax return.

Medical expenses for a child may be deducted as an itemized deduction regardless of which parent is entitled to claim the child as a dependent or who has custody of the child.

The childcare credit can be tricky. If the parents are divorced, legally separated, or live apart during the last six months of the year, the parent who has custody during the greater portion of the year is entitled to the child care credit, regardless of which parent is entitled to claim the child as a dependent. However, if the child lives with you, but your ex pays the child care provider directly, neither of you can claim the credit and it will be lost.

If you are entitled to claim the children on your return, but your ex threatens to claim them instead, file early in the year. If you've already claimed the children, the IRS will make your ex prove entitlement to the exemption.

## Filing Your Taxes Each Year

If you are employed, you should change your withholding on Form W-4 to reflect your current filing status. If you are paying tax-deductible alimony, increase your exemptions so that less in taxes is taken out of your paycheck. You can claim one exemption for every $3,000 or so of deductions, including alimony payments. If you are receiving alimony, ask to have extra tax withheld from your paycheck to cover your new tax liability.

# CHAPTER 10

# After the Divorce

Finally, your divorce is over! You are looking ahead to your new life as a single person. You're ready to close this chapter of your life and open a new one—emotionally and financially. In this section, we will cover things you need to do to handle loose ends after the divorce, and how to make good decisions now that you are on your own.

## Gather documents

### Your Divorce Decree

When your divorce is final, be sure to obtain a court-certified copy of the decree for your files. Make several copies and keep the original in your safe deposit box. You will need it in the future for a number of reasons.

- If you later seek modification of the support provisions of your decree, such as child support or alimony, you will need a copy of the decree to show the attorney, if you use one.

- If you bring a subsequent action for modification or enforcement of support in a court other than the one in which you were granted your divorce, you will probably need to file a copy of the decree with the new court.

- If you seek a wage withholding order from your ex's new employer, you will need a copy of the decree to prove the amount of support.

- If you contact your local child support collection unit, they will want to see a copy of your decree to verify the amount of support.

- If you need to enforce support in another state, you will need a copy of the final decree to file as an out-of-state order with that state.

- If you apply for a loan and pay or receive support, you may be asked to provide a copy of the final decree to prove the amount of support you pay or receive.

- If you are granted sole ownership of your residence or other real property, your mortgage company may require a copy of the final decree to transfer the mortgage to your name.

- If you seek Social Security benefits based on your ex's earnings record, you will need to send a copy to the Social Security Administration at retirement.

- Your accountant or attorney may want to see a copy of the final settlement agreement when preparing future tax returns or drafting new wills or trusts for you.

## Property Records

You will need complete records and documentation on the assets you receive as part of your divorce settlement, for two primary reasons:

- To calculate the tax basis so you can determine gain or loss for tax purposes in the event you sell the property, and

- To obtain warranty coverage or increase resale value while you hold that asset.

Get all of the records on your homes, rental properties, and investments. You will need them to calculate your tax basis, to substantiate claims, or to calculate investment return.

Also get records for your vehicles and smaller appliances. For example, get the purchase contract, warranty and service records on your car. Not only will these records be important in documenting the tax basis and resale value, but they also have important information concerning repairs. Having those records may help you cut future service costs and increase the car's resale value.

## Check your credit

As a single person, you have the right to obtain credit, and a credit report, in your own name. You can obtain a copy of your credit report from the "Big 3" credit bureaus—Experian (experian.com) at 888-397-3742, Transunion (transunion.com) at 800-888-4213 and Equifax (equifax.com) at 800-685-1111.

If you find any errors in your report, return the dispute form enclosed with your credit report. The credit bureau must attempt to verify the information your dispute. If they can't resolve the dispute within 30 days, they must remove the information from your credit report.

# Your New Goals and Objectives

## Review Your Goals

After your divorce, you are starting again with a clean slate and have a second chance to plan your future. This is an excellent time to think about your goals for the future. Do you want to go back to school? Change careers? Retire? Do you want to buy a new car, a new home, plan for retirement, or pay off debt?

Start by identifying your short-term and longer-term goals and then determine the amount needed to fulfill each goal and your timeline for doing so. With this information, you can review your investments and determine if they are appropriate to your new goals and lifestyle. Consult a financial professional for a check-up to ensure that you are putting everything on the right track.

## Review Your Budget

In divorce, the money that formerly operated one household now must run two, so cutting expenses is mandatory. Don't put off needed medical procedures, car repairs, home maintenance, or credit card payments. Rather, reduce discretionary expenses, beginning now.

Here are a few helpful ideas to make every dollar count.

- Shrink food costs by clipping coupons, buying on sale, purchasing generic brands, and buying in bulk.

- Improve your gas mileage by tuning up your car, checking the air in the tires, and driving less—carpool and combine trips instead.

- Conserve water and electricity.

- Make long distance calls only when necessary and at off-peak savings rates.

- Spend less on gifts and vacations.

- Carry your lunch to work.

- Buy secondhand furniture and appliances.

## Consider Renting

Until you are sure of your future goals, consider renting rather than buying. Closing costs, loan points, and other expenses make home purchases a costly proposition, especially if you will need to sell in a few years. Although you want to anchor yourself emotionally after divorce, rushing to purchase a new home may not anchor you—it may sink your ship. Slow down and get settled into your new life before you make important decisions such as buying a home.

As time passes, you will decide where you want to live and work. If you find you have the necessary down payment for a house, you'll still want to consider the pros and cons of buying versus renting. Consider the following in making your decision:

• How much can you save each year by paying rent rather than mortgage payments? To compute mortgage payments, figure the amount you would finance after making a down payment, then consult an amortization table at your library or on line, or use a financial calculator to figure the mortgage payment for a 30-year loan at today's interest rates. Multiply the mortgage payment by 12 to get the annual total, and then add to that amount the insurance and property taxes, and the monthly homeowner association fees, if any, multiplied by 12. If you are flush with cash, have a good monthly income and want to pay off your mortgage quickly to save interest, check into a 15-year loan. The monthly payments will be higher, but you'll save an enormous amount in interest payments.

• How much can you save each year in income taxes by buying a home rather than renting? To compute your home mortgage interest deduction, multiply the loan amount by the interest rate. Add to this amount the annual property taxes and multiply the total by your tax rate.

• If you didn't purchase a new home, how much would you earn if you had invested the money available for a down payment? Multiply the available down payment by the rate you might earn on an alternate investment. The earnings rate will probably range from the current interest rate on certificates of deposit, if you are a conservative investor, to an average growth and earnings rate on stocks and equity mutual funds, if you are more of a risk-taker.

• How much can you expect the new home to increase in value each year? Although no one can predict house appreciation, you may be able to come up with an approximate value. Consult

with Realtors and bankers to arrive at a consensus on the
anticipated annual appreciation rate. (If the general opinion is
that property in your area is declining, this may be a negative
rate rather than a positive one.) Multiply the current market
value of the new home by your estimate of the appreciation (or
depreciation) rate.

Now, add the savings of renting over buying to the lost earnings on the
down payment. Then subtract the tax savings of buying, and the anticipated annual appreciation. If the result is a positive figure, that is the
amount that you could save by renting rather than buying. If negative,
you'd be better off buying.

Even if your math shows an advantage to renting over buying, that
advantage could be short-lived. If you plan to stay in a house for a long
time, the advantages of a fixed-rate mortgage may outweigh any savings in rent, because rents generally go up over the years, while a fixed-
rate mortgage payment would stay the same. Thus the advantage of
renting over buying could evaporate in just a few years.

---

Betty and Aaron had been married for 30 years when they
divorced.

After the divorce, Betty realized that she was still in a state of
limbo. Her children were grown, but lived in a neighboring
community with their own families. She had never had a career,
but she had always wanted to pursue one. She wasn't sure what
she was going to do, where she wanted to live, or how she
wanted to spend her time.

She decided to rent a small apartment while she went back to
school to complete the education she had left off 30 years before.
After graduation, she went into the workforce and took a job
not far from her children's homes. She decided to buy a home in
that area.

A word of caution: If you plan to sell your new house in two years or less, renting will probably be better than buying. In most markets, the increase in value of your residence for the first two years will be consumed by the cost of selling the residence—commissions, title insurance, closing costs and the like. If you sell within a year or two, the appreciation in your home may be little, if anything. You may even lose money if the net sales price after commissions and expenses, is less than your original cost of the property. In general, real estate is not expected to appreciate in the future as it has in the past, so don't make your decisions on outdated assumptions.

## Life and Health Insurance

### Consider COBRA

Under COBRA (Consolidated Omnibus Budget Reconciliation Act of 1986), if your ex's company has at least 20 employees, his employer must allow you to apply to its health insurance company for continued coverage under the company plan for another three years.

The coverage is available only if the group health plan coverage was in effect for your ex at the time of divorce or legal separation, and you were covered under the plan. For example, if your ex works part-time and is not covered under the employer health plan, continuing coverage will not be available to you after divorce. Similarly, if the employer plan covers fewer than 20 employees, you may not be eligible for continuing coverage even if your ex's insurance was in effect at the time of divorce.

COBRA coverage may terminate if the employer ceases to maintain health care coverage for its employees, or if your ex fails to make timely premium payments, becomes covered under another group plan, or becomes entitled to Medicare benefits.

If you opt for COBRA coverage, at the end of three years you will either need to convert coverage to your own plan with the same company (which is likely to be considerably more expensive than the COBRA coverage) or to switch your insurance to another company.

If you have a pre-existing condition, you may not qualify for insurance at the end of the COBRA coverage. If you do qualify, the coverage is likely not to cover pre-existing conditions for the first two years you are insured, or it may be very costly. To ensure continuing coverage, consider taking out private insurance with a two-year exclusion period for your pre-existing condition within one year of beginning COBRA coverage. You will have COBRA coverage for your pre-existing illness for the three years. In addition, the two-year exclusion period will expire just as the COBRA coverage expires, leaving you fully insured under your private insurance. This is expensive, however, and you will probably want to consider it only if you cannot get a job with full coverage at a reasonable cost.

If you are healthy, consider a private plan rather than taking the COBRA coverage for three years. If you took the COBRA coverage and became ill during the three-year period, you might find that you were uninsurable at the end of three years, when the COBRA coverage expired. A private plan, rather than a group plan under COBRA, would facilitate continuing coverage and might be worth any extra expense. Private plans are usually less costly than COBRA coverage for healthy individuals.

---

Amy and Jerome divorced, leaving her with two kids, a dog, and a severe case of fibromyalgia.

Amy signed up for COBRA coverage under Jerome's insurance policy.

One year later, she bought a private insurance policy with a two-year exclusion for pre-existing conditions.

When her COBRA coverage expired three years after the divorce, Amy was able to use her private policy to cover her fibromyalgia treatments.

---

## Other Health Insurance Options

Compare the benefits and costs of various health insurance policies. To search for an individual hospitalization policy and major medical plan, consider the following sources: Blue Cross and Blue Shield, other preferred provider organizations (PPOs), health maintenance organizations (HMOs), other insurance companies, Medicare Part B and Medicare supplemental policies (if you are over 65) and group plans through professional societies and fraternal organizations of which you are a member.

When comparing policies and coverage, look for an upper limit that covers at least $1 million of medical expenses before it stops paying. Then compare initial deductibles and co-insurance clauses, to determine what portion of routine medical expenses you would end up paying. Finally, note the kinds of expenses that are excluded or limited, such as dental costs, prescription drugs, psychotherapy, pregnancy, alternative practitioners (such as chiropractors or acupuncturists), cosmetic surgery, and whatever else is important to you.

## Get Life Insurance on Your Ex

If you will depend on alimony or child support payments from your ex, get life insurance on your ex to protect your income. If the court tells your ex to keep you on his life insurance as a beneficiary until your children are grown, he must do so—even if he remarries. If he wants insurance for his new family, he will need to acquire an additional life insurance policy with his new family as the beneficiary. Before the divorce is final, make sure your ex can pass an insurance physical and will cooperate in obtaining the policy.

Remember, the policy will protect you only if it is in force when he dies, and you are the beneficiary. For that reason, insist that you be the owner of the policy, so that he cannot change the beneficiary or let the policy go into default without your knowledge. If you cannot own the policy, for example, because it is through his employment, here's what to do. Put a clause in your divorce decree that provides that he is to maintain life insurance as long as he owes support, and that if the policy is not in effect when he dies, or you are not the beneficiary, his estate will owe you the amount you should have received from the death benefits of the policy.

## Keep Your Property and Auto Insurance Current

Record the due dates for property and auto insurance premiums on your calendar, and don't assume your ex is paying the premiums; make the payments yourself. Don't remove your ex's name or assets from the policy unless you are sure your ex has obtained alternate coverage or you may be stuck with your ex's losses in the event of an uncovered claim. Also, make sure your new insurance is in place before canceling any policy, even if you may have to double up on a monthly payment.

## Revise Your Will

Once your divorce is final, you will probably want to change your will. In some states, previous beneficiary designations are void after the divorce, so even if you want to designate your ex as your heir, you must do so affirmatively after the divorce. Be sure also to change beneficiary designations where necessary for retirement plans, IRAs, life insurance, and any other assets payable in beneficiary form.

# APPENDIX A

## FINAL DIVORCE DECREE

To make sure that your final divorce decree gives you the protection that you want, use this checklist to include those items that pertain to you.

1. **The Divorce Process**
   - Who pays the legal fees?
   - Will the husband pay the legal fees and court costs if the wife must take him to court for non-support or for not complying with the divorce decree? Will there be interest charges?

2. **Property**
   - Who gets which property?
   - Who gets which debt?
   - If the pension is to be divided, has the proper paperwork been prepared?
   - If there is a property settlement note, is it collaterallized? Is there interest on it?
   - If you continue to own the house jointly, who will be responsible for paying the mortgage and other expenses?
   - If you get the house and need to sell it immediately, will you be responsible for the entire capital gains tax?

3. **Maintenance/Alimony**
   - How much maintenance for how long?
   - If maintenance is not awarded now, can it be awarded later?
   - Will there be life insurance to cover maintenance in the event of the payor's death?

4. **Child Support**
   - How much child support for how long?
   - Will the child support change during college or when visitation times change?
   - Who has custody of the children?
   - What is the visitation schedule?
   - Who pays related expenses for school (transportation, books, etc.) and unusual expenses (lessons, camp, teeth, etc.)?
   - Who will deduct the children on income tax forms?

# APPENDIX B

## CHECKLIST OF INFORMATION
## TO GATHER FOR ATTORNEY

- ❏ Name, address and phone number
- ❏ Business address and phone number
- ❏ Name, address and phone number of other party
- ❏ Dates of birth of each party
- ❏ Names and dates of birth of children
- ❏ Prior marriages of each party and details of termination
- ❏ Children of prior marriages and custodial arrangements
- ❏ Date and place of marriage
- ❏ Length of time you have lived in this state
- ❏ Name and address of lawyer representing other party
- ❏ Existence of prenuptial agreement
- ❏ Grounds for divorce
- ❏ Objectives of each party
- ❏ Date of separation
- ❏ Current employment and income of the parties
- ❏ Education/degrees/training of each party
- ❏ Job history and income potential of each party
- ❏ Employee benefits of each party
- ❏ Retirement or pension plans for each party
- ❏ Joint assets of the parties
- ❏ Liabilities or debt of each party
- ❏ Life insurance of each party
- ❏ Separate or personal assets of each party
- ❏ Incidences of domestic abuse or threats
- ❏ Financial records which include:
    - ❏ Bank statements
    - ❏ Tax returns
    - ❏ Applications for loans
    - ❏ Investment statements

❏ Family business records which include:
    ❏ Type of business
    ❏ Shareholders
    ❏ Percent of ownership of business
    ❏ Bank statements of business
    ❏ Tax returns of business
    ❏ Applications for loans
    ❏ Income and balance sheets
    ❏ Financial reports

# APPENDIX C
## ALIMONY/SPOUSAL SUPPORT FACTORS

| STATE | Statutory List | Marital Fault Not Considered | Marital Fault Relevant | Standard of Living | Status as Custodial Parent |
|---|---|---|---|---|---|
| Alabama | | | X | X | |
| Alaska | X | X | | X | X |
| Arizona | X | X | X[1] | X | X |
| Arkansas | | X | | | |
| California | X | X | | X | |
| Colorado | X | X | | X | X |
| Connecticut | X | | X | X | X |
| Delaware | X | X | | X | X |
| D.C. | | | X | X | |
| Florida | X | | X | X | |
| Georgia | X | | X | X | |
| Hawaii | X | X | | X | X |
| Idaho | X | | X | | |
| Illinois | X | X | | X | X |
| Indiana | X | X | | X | X |
| Iowa | X | X | | X | X |
| Kansas | | X | | | |
| Kentucky | X | | X[2] | X | |
| Louisiana | X | | X | | X |
| Maine | X | X | | | |
| Maryland | X | | X | X | |
| Massachusetts | X | | X | X | X |
| Michigan | | | X | X | |
| Minnesota | X | X | | X | X |
| Mississippi | | | X | | |
| Missouri | X | | X | X | X |
| Montana | X | X | | X | X |
| Nebraska | | X | | | |
| Nevada | | | X | X | X |
| New Hampshire | X | | X | X | X |
| New Jersey | X | | X | X | X |

| STATE | Statutory List | Marital Fault Not Considered | Marital Fault Relevant | Standard of Living | Status as Custodial Parent |
|---|---|---|---|---|---|
| New Mexico | X | X | | X | |
| New York | X | | X | X | X |
| North Carolina | X | X | | X | |
| North Dakota | | | X | X | |
| Ohio | X | X | | | |
| Oklahoma | | X | | X | X |
| Oregon | X | X | | X | X |
| Pennsylvania | X | | X | X | |
| Rhode Island | X | | X | X | X |
| South Carolina | X | | X | X | X |
| South Dakota | | | X | X | |
| Tennessee | X | | X | X | X |
| Texas | X | | X | X | X |
| Utah | X | | X | X | |
| Vermont | X | X | | X | X |
| Virginia | X | | X | X | |
| Washington | X | X | | X | |
| West Virginia | X | X | X | | X |
| Wisconsin | X | X | | X | X |
| Wyoming | | | X | | |

[1]Dissipation of assets is considered as a factor only if the spouse qualifies for spousal maintenance in the first place.
[2]Only fault on the part of the party seeking alimony.

# APPENDIX D
## CUSTODY CRITERIA

| STATE | Statutory Guide-lines | Children's Wishes | Joint Custody Laws | Coop-erative Parent | Domestic Violence | Health | Attorney or GAL |
|---|---|---|---|---|---|---|---|
| Alabama | | X | X | | X | | |
| Alaska | X | X | X | X | X | X | X |
| Arizona | X | X | X | X | X | X | X |
| Arkansas | | | | | | | |
| California | X | X | | | X | | X |
| Colorado | X | X | X | X | X | X | X |
| Connecticut | | X | X | | | | X |
| Delaware | X | X | | | | X | X |
| D.C. | X | X | X | X | X | X | X |
| Florida | X | X | X | X | X | X | X |
| Georgia | X | X | X | | X | | X |
| Hawaii | X | X | | | X | | X |
| Idaho | X | X | X | | X | X | |
| Illinois | X | X | X | X | X | X | X |
| Indiana | X | X | X | X | X | X | X |
| Iowa | X | X | X | X | X | X | X |
| Kansas | X | X | X | X | X | X | |
| Kentucky | X | X | X | X | X | X | X |
| Louisiana | X | X | X | | X | | |
| Maine | X | X[1] | X[2] | | X | | X |
| Maryland | | | X | | X | | X |
| Massachusetts | | | X | | X | | X |
| Michigan | X | X | X | X | X | X | X |
| Minnesota | X | X | X | | X | X | X |
| Mississippi | X | | X | | | | |
| Missouri | X | X | X | X | X | X | X |
| Montana | X | X | X[3] | | X | | X |
| Nebraska | X | X | X | | | X | X |
| Nevada | X | X | X | X | X | | X |
| New Hampshire | X | X | X | | X | | X |
| New Jersey | X | X | X | X | X | X | X |
| New Mexico | X | X | X | X | X | X | X |

122

| STATE | Statutory Guidelines | Children's Wishes | Joint Custody Laws | Cooperative Parent | Domestic Violence | Health | Attorney or GAL |
|---|---|---|---|---|---|---|---|
| New York | | X | | | | | X |
| North Carolina | | X | | | X | X | |
| North Dakota | X | X | | X[4] | X | X | |
| Ohio | X | X | X[5] | | X | X | X |
| Oklahoma | X | X | X | X | X | | |
| Oregon | X | X | X | X | X | | X |
| Pennsylvania | X | X | X | X | X | X | X |
| Rhode Island | | X | X | X | X | X | X |
| South Carolina | | X | X | X | X | X | X |
| South Dakota | | X | X | X | X | | |
| Tennessee | X | X | X | | X | X | X |
| Texas | X | X | X | X | X | X | X |
| Utah | X | X | X | X | | | X |
| Vermont | X | | X | | X | | X |
| Virginia | X | X | X | X | X | X | X |
| Washington | X | X[6] | | | X | X | X |
| West Virginia | | X | X | | X | | |
| Wisconsin | X | X | X | X | X | X | X |
| Wyoming | | X | X | | X | | |

[1]Considered if child is old enough.
[2]Now uses term *shared parental rights and responsibilities*.
[3]Now uses term *parenting* and "joint" language has been eliminated.
[4]By case law.
[5]Now called *shared parenting*.
[6]At discretion of court.

# APPENDIX E
## CHILD SUPPORT GUIDELINES

| | Income Share | Percent of Income | Extraordinary Medical Add On | Child-care Add On | College Support | UIFSA |
|---|---|---|---|---|---|---|
| Alabama | X | | X | X | X | |
| Alaska | | X | X | | | X |
| Arizona | X | | X | X | | X |
| Arkansas | | X | | | | X |
| California | X | | X | X | | |
| Colorado | X | | | X | X | X |
| Connecticut | X | | | | | |
| Delaware | | | X | X | | X |
| D.C. | | X | X[1] | X | X[2] | X |
| Florida | X | | X | X | | X |
| Georgia | | X | X | X | | |
| Hawaii | | | | X | X | X |
| Idaho | X | | X | X | | X |
| Illinois | | X | | | X | X |
| Indiana | X | | X | X | X | X |
| Iowa | | X | | | X | X |
| Kansas | X | | X | X | | X |
| Kentucky | X | | X | X | | |
| Louisiana | X | | X | X | | X |
| Maine | X | | X | X | | X |
| Maryland | X | | X | X | | X |
| Massachusetts | | X | X | | X | X |
| Michigan | X | | X | X | X | X |
| Minnesota | | X | | X | | X |
| Mississippi | | X | | | | |
| Missouri | X | | X | X | X | X |
| Montana | | | X | X | | X |
| Nebraska | X | | | X | | X |
| Nevada | | X | X | | | X |
| New Hampshire | | X | | | X | X |
| New Jersey | X | | X | X | X | |

| STATE | Income Share | Percent of Income | Extraordinary Medical Add On | Child-care Add On | College Support | UIFSA |
|---|---|---|---|---|---|---|
| New Mexico | X | | X | X | | X |
| New York | X | | X | X | X | |
| North Carolina | X | | X | X | | X |
| North Dakota | | X | | X | | X |
| Ohio | X | | | X | | |
| Oklahoma | X | | X | X | | X |
| Oregon | X | | X | X | X | X |
| Pennsylvania | X | | X | X | | X |
| Rhode Island | X | | | X | | X |
| South Carolina | X | | X | X | X | X |
| South Dakota | X | X | X | X | | X |
| Tennessee | | X | | | | |
| Texas | | X | X | | | X |
| Utah | X | | X | X | | X |
| Vermont | X | | X | X | | |
| Virginia | X | | X | X | | X |
| Washington | X | | X | X | X | X |
| West Virginia | X | | X | X | | |
| Wisconsin | | X | X | | | X |
| Wyoming | X | | | | | X |

[1]Some latitude to consider extraordinary medical expenses in setting obligor's support requirement.
[2]Support is to age twenty-one, and college expenses could be a factor used to vary the percentage of income for support.

# APPENDIX F
## GROUNDS FOR DIVORCE AND RESIDENCY REQUIREMENTS

| STATE | No Fault Sole Ground | No Fault Added to Traditional | Incom-patibility | Living Separate & Apart | Judicial Separation | Durational Requirements |
|---|---|---|---|---|---|---|
| Alabama | | X | X | 2 years | X | 6 months |
| Alaska | | X | X | | X | None |
| Arizona | X | | | | X | 90 days |
| Arkansas | | X | | 18 mths | X | 60 days |
| California | X | | | | X | 6 months |
| Colorado | X | | | | X | 90 days |
| Connecticut | | X | | 18 mths | X | 1 year |
| Delaware | X | | | | | 6 months |
| D.C. | X | | | 1 year | X | 6 months |
| Florida | X | | | | | 6 months |
| Georgia | | X | | | | 6 months |
| Hawaii | X | | | 2 years | X | 6 months |
| Idaho | | X | | | X | 6 weeks |
| Illinois | | X | | 2 years | X | 90 days |
| Indiana | | X | | | X | 60 days |
| Iowa | X | | | | X | None |
| Kansas | | | X | | | 60 days |
| Kentucky | X | | | | X | 180 days |
| Louisiana | | X | | 6 mths | X | None |
| Maine | | X | | | X | 6 months |
| Maryland | | X | | 2 years | X | 1 year |
| Massachusetts | | X | | | X | None |
| Michigan | X | | | | X | 6 months |
| Minnesota | X | | | | X | 180 days[1] |
| Mississippi | | X | X[2] | | | 6 months |
| Missouri | | X | | 1-2 yrs | X | 90 days |
| Montana | X | | X | 180 days | X | 90 days |
| Nebraska | X | | | | X | 1 year |
| Nevada | | | X | 1 year | X | 6 weeks |
| New Hampshire | | X | | 2 years | | 1 year |

126

| STATE | No Fault Sole Ground | No Fault Added to Traditional | Incompatibility | Living Separate & Apart | Judicial Separation | Durational Requirements |
|---|---|---|---|---|---|---|
| New Jersey | | X | | 18 mths | | 1 year |
| New Mexico | | X | X | | X | 6 months |
| New York | | X | | 1 year | X | 1 year |
| North Carolina | | | | 1 year | X | 6 months |
| North Dakota | | X | | | X | 6 months |
| Ohio | | X | X | 1 year | | 6 months |
| Oklahoma | | X | X | | X | 6 months |
| Oregon | X | | | | X | 6 months |
| Pennsylvania | | X | | 2 years | | 6 months |
| Rhode Island | | X | | 3 years | X | 1 year |
| South Carolina | | X | | 1 year | X | 3 months (both residents) |
| South Dakota | | X[3] | | | X | None |
| Tennessee | | X | | 2 years | X | 6 months |
| Texas | | X | | 3 years | | 6 months |
| Utah | | X | | 3 years | X | 90 days |
| Vermont | | X | | 6 mths | | 6 months |
| Virginia | | X | | 1 year | | 6 months |
| Washington | X | | | | | 1 year |
| West Virginia | | X | | 1 year | X | 1 year |
| Wisconsin | X | | | | X | 6 months |
| Wyoming | X | | X | | X | 60 days |

[1] 180 days for Minnesota jurisdiction to hear divorce case; does not relate to grounds.
[2] Irretrievable breakdown.
[3] No fault ground only available if parties agree or in a default situation.

## PROPERTY DIVISION

| STATE | Community Property | Only Marital Divided | Statutory List of Factors | Non-Monetary Contributions | Economic Misconduct | Contribution to Education |
|---|---|---|---|---|---|---|
| Alabama | | X | | X | | X |
| Alaska | | X | | X | X | X |
| Arizona | X | | X | | X | X[1] |
| Arkansas | | X | X | X | | |
| California | X | | X | X | X | X |
| Colorado | | X | X | X | X | |
| Connecticut | | | X | X | X | X |
| Delaware | | | X | X | X | |
| D.C. | | X | X | X | X | |
| Florida | | X | X | X | X | X |
| Georgia | | X | | | | |
| Hawaii | | | X | X | X | |
| Idaho | X | | X | | | |
| Illinois | | X | X | X | X | |
| Indiana | | X | X | X | X | X |
| Iowa | | X | X | X | | |
| Kansas | | | X | | X | |
| Kentucky | | X | X | X | X | X |
| Louisiana | X | | | | | |
| Maine | | X | X | X | X | |
| Maryland | | X | X | X | | |
| Massachusetts | | | X | X | X | |
| Michigan | | X | | X | X | X |
| Minnesota | | X[2] | X | X | X | |
| Mississippi | | X | | X | X | X |
| Missouri | | X | X | X | X | X |
| Montana | | | X | X | X | |
| Nebraska | | X | | X | | |
| Nevada | X | X | | X | X | X |
| New Hampshire | | | X | X | X | X |
| New Jersey | | X | X | X | X | X |
| New Mexico | X | | | | | |

| STATE | Community Property | Only Marital Divided | Statutory List of Factors | Non-Monetary Contributions | Economic Misconduct | Contribution to Education |
|---|---|---|---|---|---|---|
| New York | | X | X | X | X | X |
| North Carolina | | X | X | X | X | X |
| North Dakota | | | | X | X | X |
| Ohio | | X | X | X | X | X |
| Oklahoma | | X | | X | X | |
| Oregon | | | | X | X | X |
| Pennsylvania | | X | X | X | X | X |
| Rhode Island | | X | X | X | X | X |
| South Carolina | | X | X | X | X | X |
| South Dakota | | | | X | X | |
| Tennessee | | X | X | X | X | X |
| Texas | X | | | | X | |
| Utah | | | | | X | |
| Vermont | | | X | X | X | X |
| Virginia | | X | X | X | X | |
| Washington | X | | X | | | |
| West Virginia | | X | X | X | X | X |
| Wisconsin | X | X | X | X | X | X |
| Wyoming | | X | X | | | |

[1]Contribution to education is a spousal maintenance factor. One case provides restitution if a spouse makes extraordinary unilateral efforts resulting in another's education.
[2]Nonmarital may be invaded up to 50 percent unfair hardship.

Source: ©The American Bar Association. All rights reserved.
Reprinted by Permission of ABA Publishing: All tables are current as of March 2002.
http://www.abanet.org/family/familylaw/tables.html.

# HOW A CERTIFIED DIVORCE SPECIALIST CAN HELP YOU

According to divorce experts, what's missing in most divorce processes is financial expertise. Certified Divorce Specialists using **DivorcePro™** software go a long way toward filling that need.

Carol Ann Wilson is a Certified Financial Planner and a Certified Divorce Specialist, and co-author of this book. She developed **DivorcePro™** software which accounts for all financial assets of the couple and creates a number of scenarios to show how every decision affects both parties for years to come. An easy-to-understand set of graphs shows how each spouse's income and assets change over time.

This system allows both partners, as well as the judge, to have a clearer view of their financial futures.

Example: A single-income divorce

Ted and Sue are 40 years old and have 2 children. They own a home worth $280,000 with net equity of $132,000. Their IRAs and 401k plan total $86,000 in value. Ted's take-home pay is $68,760 a year.

This is the settlement originally proposed. After the divorce, Sue and the children will live in the house, which will be deeded to her. She will also receive $86,000 of the retirement moneys and Ted will get the remaining $218,000 thus dividing the assets equally. Ted will pay Sue alimony of $1,450 per month for 5 years and $550 per month child support. He will also pay college costs which start in 4 years. Sue earns $18,000 per year.

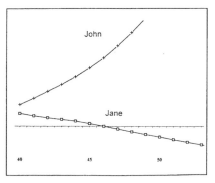

At first glance this looks like a fair settlement. But the graph tells a different story. Within ten years, Sue's assets will be depleted while Ted's net worth has grown dramatically. (See Figure 1.)

The **DivorcePro**™ Proposal

**DivorcePro**™ projections suggest higher alimony for a longer period of time and a disproportional split of assets, combined with lowered expense for Sue. Ted is still able to increase his net worth. This scenario would result in an equitable financial situation for both parties. (See Figure 2.)

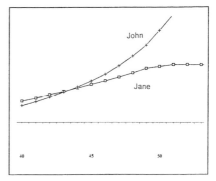

### What is a Certified Divorce Specialist?
A Certified Divorce Specialist (CDS), can be a lawyer, financial planner, accountant or any other financial professional who has completed the specialized training in the financial issues of divorce through the College for Divorce Specialists. A CDS must also fulfill the continuing education requirements and adhere to the Code of Ethics described through the College for Divorce Specialists.

A CDS takes all of the financial issues into consideration and by using Divorce Pro™, a specialized software program, shows the long-term financial results of any given proposed divorce settlement.

For the name of a Certified Divorce Specialist near you, go to *www.cdsCollege.com* or call tollfree: 1-866-527-3193.

**College for Divorce Specialists**
**6395 Gunpark Drive, Suite Y**
**Boulder, CO 80301**
**303-527-3193**
**tollfree: 1-866-527-3193**
**www.cdsCollege.com**